GROWING UP
SICK

HOW TO TURN YOUR KID'S SCARY
DIAGNOSIS INTO A HIGH-QUALITY LIFE

Lauren B. Weeks

Lauren B. Weeks 1st edition 2018

Copyright © Lauren Bombardier Weeks
ISBN: 978-1-7323801-1-0 (ebook)
ISBN: 978-1-7323801-0-3 (Paperback)
ISBN: 978-1-7323801-2-7 (Hardcover)

http://thesowhatlife.com

Cover Design by Fiction-Atlas Press LLC http://fiction-atlas.com

Formatting by Polgarus Studio http://polgarusstudio.com

Contents

Introduction

My mom is a force. As a nurse, she's seen it all. So naturally, growing up, my brothers and I could complain about very little. Skinned your knee? Some hot soapy water, a Band-Aid, and a kiss, and we were back out playing with our friends. Bellyache? Take some Pepto-Bismol and eat your dinner. Have a cold? Drink some water and take a nap.

Everyone calls my mom when they have an issue they need solving. Usually, it's a medical issue, and most of the time she'll confirm that no, they aren't dying, they are probably just constipated, dehydrated, or stressed out. Other times, she'll spring into action and be there for cancer diagnoses, broken legs, and heart attacks. She's been at the bedside of a dying neighbor on more than one occasion, always knows the right thing to say when it happens, and is sure to send flowers and a card right away.

So when my nine-year-old brother brought home head lice from elementary school to share with me and my seven-year-old brother, the world didn't end. Before she realized he had the little bugs crawling around his head, my mom, brothers, and I were snuggled in bed watching TGIF on ABC, the jokes going straight over my three-year-old head, while Dad worked second shift. My brothers bounced around on the bed, and I yelled at them to get out of the way of the TV. The lice spread quickly, and now she had not one, but three kids with head lice.

We sat around the kitchen table, as she patiently combed through our hair with a magnifying glass. What parent wants to be surrounded by kids who have nasty, creepy head lice? My mom was a pro and relished in her ability to kill the suckers. She was exhausted, but kept a smile on her face while my brothers kicked each other under the table, and while I whined that she was pulling my hair (which was cut short because I whined when anyone brushed through it).

* * *

It had been a long drive home from Children's Hospital earlier that afternoon. Mom pointed out the Whale Mural on 93 South coming back from Boston, and I ogled out the back window.

"Dad! Is that how big they are?"

He laughed, and told me what kind of whale it was, as if I would remember. To this day, he has always been always filled with facts about animals, plants, you name it.

At the hospital that day, I was focused on my roller-skating doll, holding onto her long, ratty hair so she could skate down the tile hallway. While my parents stopped at the front desk to ask how to get to the pulmonary department, I stared at the frog statue in the fountain, hoping my mom would give me a penny to throw in.

That day, my mom and dad received the news they feared: Their daughter had cystic fibrosis.

And there I was, standing in front of them, a smiling 3-year-old with a raspy voice and a two-note cough, asking when Santa was coming. I had no idea the hand I had just been dealt. And there was my mom, who was usually the one doling out medical advice, faced with a devastating diagnosis she knew little about.

* * *

When Mom called my grandma to tell her our family wouldn't be coming to Christmas Eve, due to the lice, Grandma responded in her caring way, "Lee, this Christmas you need to be with your family. I don't care if the kids have lice."

And so, we walked through the door of the ham-and-pine-scented old home, Dad's arms filled with presents, the shouts and giggles of our 20 or so cousins echoing throughout the hallway. The boys were roughhousing, their hair trimmed short, and the girls played with their dolls, their own hair in tight braids. Mom laughed at the thought of Dad's siblings carefully shaving off their boys' hair, and tightly pulling up the girls' locks.

It was Christmas, and I, the raspy voiced 3-year-old, just wanted to play with my dolls and my cousins, and look for Rudolph's red nose in the night sky. So what if what I pointed out in the sky was actually an airplane getting ready to land at Logan Airport?

Mom and Dad tucked us in that Christmas Eve and told us they loved us. While I lay in bed, nervous about this Santa guy who'd be coming tonight, my parents lay together, nervous about my short life. Mom and Dad talked about what life would be like for me, their little girl, who was just diagnosed with this scary illness. And eventually, they decided they would just let me live. Like they did when we skinned our knees, like they did that Christmas Eve, as I coughed away, playing with my dolls, scratching my lice-covered head.

And boy... THANK GOD they did. Unbeknownst to my parents, they made an important decision that affected the way I would live my life through adulthood. Growing up, I figured out pretty quickly that life must go on. It had to. And luckily, it meant I could still have fun, laugh, and dance (so much dancing) even when I felt like doodie, or was bummed out.

I'm the author of the blog, *The So What Life*, which is all about my life with cystic fibrosis, the lessons I've learned, the heartache I've experienced, and most of all, the crazy appreciation I've gained for my life. I've spoken to dozens of parents throughout the years who are in the exact same position my parents were over 20 years ago. Maybe I'm introduced to them as a representation of who their child could be in 20 years, but mostly, I remind them that they aren't alone, that this isn't going to be easy, and that now's the time to make the conscious decision to give their child the quality of life I had.

Whenever my blog comes up in conversation, people say, "I don't know how you do it. How do you stay so strong?" And I always shrug my shoulders and say, "My parents never made cf a big deal, so I never realized it was so special to be strong." To be honest, sometimes I don't feel like I'm all that brave, I'm just living my life the only way I know how. And I've never really known anything different.

I don't have a PhD in psychology, I'm not a parent, and I'm not giving you any peer-reviewed studies about the most well-researched way of raising children. What I am is realistic. What I am is a success story. I'm a well-adjusted adult, who had a happy childhood which happened to be filled with some pretty shitty stuff by an average person's definition. I'll tell you my observations of the world, sometimes bluntly, in the hopes that you can take something away from it.

Over the years, I've noticed that the rhetoric around raising a child with a chronic illness, a disability, or any life-altering tragedy, is so *freaking* sad. It's exhausting how sad it is. It's nothing like that Christmas with my lice-avoiding cousins, blissfully unaware of the disease chomping away at my body.

The rhetoric out there is all about taking care of yourself, taking care of your child, the emotional toll it has on families, on relationships, on your kid, how to prevent those tolls, how to keep your child alive, and how to keep yourself sane. Ugh. And worst of all, there's no manual that tells you what's about to happen, so parents begin to Google the fate of anyone who has dealt with the same diagnosis as their child, and it's hardly ever positive.

No lie, one parent of a child with cf was actually told by her child's doctor to go home and Google cystic fibrosis. Oh boy. When you do that, you fall into the black hole of the internet, a place without the heart to say, "You're going through a lot right now, let's give you some hope." Instead, you find facts. Cold facts, with no emotion or hope behind their words. You might find pages filled with prayers, and thinking-of-yous, and, "I just can't imagine..." Trust me, I've yet to find someone who has Googled their disease and found something inspiring.

In 1993, when I was diagnosed, we didn't have a computer. All my mom knew she learned in nursing school: Kids who had cf died, and they died young. How did anyone live without being able to connect with random strangers online? By the late 90's she had the power of the internet, and the unfortunate downfall: The stories of people not doing well, of parents going through immense heartache, and the people who just needed to vent about how horrible it all was. My dad would find her buried in our Gateway 2000 and say, "Uh oh. Lee, I think it's time to sign off!" Thank God someone was sane enough to pull her away from the negativity vortex!

But she knew that this would take a toll on her and our family, that the life expectancy for kids with cf wasn't all that promising at the time. Nothing on those websites was able to slap her and tell her she had better make a decision about how her daughter's life was gonna go. Thankfully, she came to it on her own, but in the midst of all of that sadness, it's easy, *so* easy, to fall into the trap: The primal urge to protect your child from all the bad in the world, to do everything you can to prevent them from meeting the fate of all those dead or sick people online, and to get super bummed out about it. There are two ways of doing this. One is a trap, the other is a decision, and it's a decision I'm lucky my mom and dad made.

1) You protect your child from every germ, every side effect, every bit of pain, reality, and any bit of discomfort. This takes many forms: Disinfecting every little spot they touch, keeping them out of school, changing the way you make decisions because of their unique situation, hiding the truth, fighting with them to take their pills or whatever treatment they've been prescribed, feeling exasperated when they won't listen, not letting them get dirty, make mistakes, and be imperfect like children tend to be. Okay, the cat's out of the bag. This one is the trap.

OR

2) You love your child. You love them through the sleepless nights, the scary tears, the tough conversations about life and death, through the grumpy arguments about their health, despite their mistakes, their imperfections, and their sadness. You tell them when they're being a pain in the butt and using their disease as an excuse, and sometimes you give

them a pity party when it's really warranted. You fight for your child. You raise money or awareness for their illness, and you tell them why: It's for them, because you love them. You let them get dirty, yell at them for ruining their new pair of jeans, and you're there to run a soapy tub when they come inside. You let them cry, and you're there to giggle at the snot dribbling down their nose. And you laugh with them, at the not-so-glamorous aspects of their illness (for me that's my stinky farts! And no one laughs harder than my mom when I hotbox the car). You recognize that this diagnosis is going to affect their life immensely, so you decide to allow them to live that life with zest and without barriers.

What those books and sad stories online don't tell you is that the second option *always* results in a better life for your kid (and frankly, yourself too), even if your definition of a "good life" might be different from theirs. This book isn't about saving your child's life or keeping them alive. I'm sorry to tell you I don't have any secrets to a longer life, or for curing the painful symptoms they may be experiencing. What I do have is the secret to giving your child the *best* life possible, and to living a positive life rather than one wrought with negativity. Quality over quantity.

Of course, as a parent, you want to protect your child from the bad, but we forget there's a child whose life is going to be changed for better or for worse by their special situation. And unless their parents, and the people who care for those kids, make the conscious decision to allow them to live their life with no excuses, from day one, that child's quality of life will suffer. Period. The kid already has to deal with a possible lifetime of chronic illness; the last thing they need in that moment is to be limited in anything else in their life, or to grow up with a bad attitude.

Lucky for you, I have a secret no one told my parents when I was a kid, and that most parents of kids with chronic illnesses/disabilities rarely hear.

Your kid…

- …is going to have the most unique perspective of the world. It might be a little weird to you, but it's how they'll grow and mature.

- …is going to grow up appreciating life. They're going to laugh at things you never knew could be funny, and you're going to learn to appreciate those moments.
- …is going to mature faster than their peers, will be tougher than most of them, and will teach you more than you could ever teach them.
- …is going to inspire you, every single day.

All of this will be true if you give them a **quality** life. And everything in this book will teach you what that means and how to do it, whether they're newly diagnosed, young and moldable, have had this illness for a while, or they're a pre-teen or teenager and are seemingly horrible (I was). What follows are the most valuable lessons my parents taught me, the ones that led me to be a responsible adult—someone who takes care of herself, enjoys life, and isn't afraid of the future, but accepts the present as it is.

Drug Trials

"Can you please hold?"

I hold my breath, my hands gripping the steering wheel on the way home to my apartment.

This hold is not like other holds where you twirl your pencil, click through your emails, cover the receiver and whisper to your friend. It isn't the type of hold where you get that jazzy hold music and bob your head and tap your foot, even though you're pissed they put you on hold. No, this hold will choose my fate.

This is the hold I have been waiting for for nearly ten years. I have wished for this hold on every birthday candle—the wish that springs into my head before I have a chance to think of money, love, or a new dog—some version of "I wish for more time." Despite the fact that life is seemingly flying by, closer and closer to the median life expectancy of someone with cystic fibrosis, this hold lasts a century.

When I was in middle school, my parents took out a home equity loan to build an addition on our house. What began as an idea to build a screened-in porch, turned into a four-season sun room addition. They wanted a place away from the TV, where they could relax and host friends. After weeks of builders coming in and out of the house, it was finally complete. New furniture was delivered, inspiring quotes were nailed to the walls, and Dad positioned a bird feeder right outside the far corner window.

Some days, I escaped to the "new room" to do homework, closing the

French double doors. Inevitably, though, I ended up on Facebook. On this particular day, a friend with cf shared an article about two new medications, vx-770 and vx-809. "The combination of vx-770 and vx-809 has the potential to treat the underlying cause of cystic fibrosis in those with the Delta F-508 mutation." This is my mutation. It would thin my mucus, help me gain weight, and make my damaged salt channels function again. My future, which, in the timeline in my head had a bold dark line around the year 2022, suddenly becomes a blurred expanse, the hazy horizon of a desert, the sky beyond the clouds, the ground beneath the grass. You can't see it, but you know it's there. Up until now, my life was like the minute hand of a broken watch, unwillingly ticking in place.

Looking out at the birds flocking around a rogue squirrel, I cry big wet soppy tears. The kind that careen down into your mouth like flooded rivers in spring. College. My own dog. A career. A family of my own. Cooking my own pancakes on Sunday morning in my own house.

But the trials would take years. I go straight to Google. "How many years does a drug take to be approved?" The results populate and I click on the first link. Ten, sometimes fifteen years, *if* it even makes it. It will spend time in safety trials, then some more in humans. It will be years before we know if it really works. I am 16. The median life expectancy for people with cf is 32. I am halfway there. The clock is still stuck.

So I do my best estimating. The drug is already in human trials, so that knocks off a couple years. I google more questions about trials that take too long, FDA approvals, and come up with a range. If all goes well, this drug will be in my hands after I graduate from college. I just have to make it through without any major complications. Talk about racing time. It's me verses cf, baby!

You've probably noticed that I don't capitalize "cf" and I will continue to break this grammar rule throughout the book. You might wonder why. Well, I had a creative writing teacher in high school who crossed out "CF" in a poem and wrote "Don't capitalize it, it doesn't deserve to be capitalized."

And here's why. Cystic fibrosis (cf) causes a defect in the protein that keeps your organs hydrated. You know that sheen you see on organs in medical TV shows? My sheen is a thick, yellow mucus. Mainly, this causes issues in my lungs. Have you ever had a really bad cold and coughed up phlegm? That's what's in my lungs. Only worse. See, when that phlegm sits there your whole life, it gets infected. Lungs like mine are the perfect home for pseudomonas, burkholderia cepacia, Methicillin-resistant Staphylococcus aureus. I swear the scientists who named these things thought of the most intimidating sounding names to match how intimidating it is to find out they've become squatters in your lungs—uninvited and impossible to evict.

As your body tries to fight off that chronic infection day by day, you get worn out. Fevers, fatigue, painful scarring, and inflammation are as normal as your grandpa falling asleep during Wheel of Fortune, and snoring through Final Jeopardy. Eventually, cf gets so bad that you all but drown in your own phlegm. Sexy, huh?

So, in order to get that mucus out, I have a couple options. One is chest physical therapy (Chest PT). Another person pounds on my back like they are playing the bongos, only with cupped hands and without a joint in their mouth. Trust me, if the person doesn't cup their hands, it's like getting slapped over and over again, and you didn't even diss your girlfriend to deserve it. My other option is a therapy vest. When I was around 7, some genius invented a machine that expels the mucus a different way: by filling up a vest that looks like a hollow life jacket with air, and making it vibrate through hoses connected into an air compressor. While the therapy vest meant I didn't need Dad to play the bongos on my back, it still meant I was attached to a machine daily, and made treatment time a bit more lonely. It also wasn't as rigorous as the hard clapping my dad could do. Still, it freed him up to get my brothers ready for school, and gave me the power to take charge of my treatments when I wanted to do them, not just when my dad was available. To this day, I plug myself into the vest and sit alone every morning, evicting the mucus out of my lungs.

And this is just how cf affects me on a good day. When the infection becomes too much for my body to fight off, and the mucus builds up in my lungs and crusts over, I intervene more harshly. Most of the time, this means I'll spend two or three weeks in the hospital, or at home, infusing some pretty strong drugs—the kind that weaken the bacteria while simultaneously weakening everything else in my body—and undergoing some intense chest physical therapy from the professionals: physical therapists, who play whack-a-mole on my ribs a few times a day.

While most of my medications weaken the scary bacteria, or break up the mucus, vx-809 would go one step further: it would correct the very defect in my genetic makeup, the mutated CFTR protein that kept my sodium channels from working properly—the protein that created mucus, rather than the slippery, thin stuff meant to keep my organs hydrated. Lauren without mucus would be as drastic a change as Lauren without a constant desire to eat chicken nuggets. This drug would be life-changing, unimaginable, and a shift away from something that had affected my life so consistently, that I had never imagined what life might be like without it.

Today, I wait on hold to find out if insurance will approve the $400,000 medication, approved by the FDA one week ago.

What I didn't know then, sitting in the corner of the "new room" watching the birds and sobbing like I just won a Grammy, is that those years I counted on my fingers would mold me and make me come to the most important realization about my life. And maybe, I needed those years.

Wasted Time

With each breath comes another sob. My lungs constrict, my heart rate speeds up, and I clench my jaw.

"I can't do it. It hurts too much," I manage.

It's not raining like it should be. He's staring out the window of his old, gray, busted up Dodge Caravan. The sun is shining, bouncing light off the waves in front of us. I wish we were sitting in the sand, watching the waves come in instead of sitting in this van crying. I'm squinting through my tears, trying to make out the expression on his face. At first, I think it's concern. But then I realize it is fear. I cough. Abdominal muscles tightening, body convulsing with each forceful huff, the cough keeps coming and coming, a result of all of the stress my body is under.

So *this* is what it feels like for your heart to break. Sure, the pain in the middle of my chest makes sense… but what about the pain in my lungs? I realize I read his face all wrong. He isn't afraid. I am. He can move on with his life; the scar tissue on his heart will heal. And so will mine, with time. But my lungs will still hurt; these coughing attacks will continue for the rest of my life. I'll need someone to hold onto. He won't.

"Mike, I can't just take almost five years of my life and throw it away."

I see the clock skip.

He looks at me with those green eyes that say so much when he is too nervous to say what he means.

"What we had was special, Lauren. You know that."

"Then why give up? Why now?"

"Because we're going into a new phase of our lives. I think it's just time to let go."

"But I love you."

"And I love you. That's why I have to let you go."

It doesn't make sense to me. Why would you let someone you care so much about go? How could I go on living without him? Who would I call when I was sick and afraid? Who would hug me to make me feel better?

He turns his head and looks at me from the corner of his eye for just one second.

Words too scary to be said with eye contact.

"Promise me you'll take care of yourself."

I inhale and sigh, unsure if it's possible. I think of my mom and dad, who trained me to be independent.

"Of course."

He leans over for a hug and I bury myself in his arms, inhaling the scent of his cheap cologne. I cry. But he remains strong. I think of my favorite poem, Sonnet 116, by William Shakespeare:

"Love is not love

Which alters when it alteration finds,

Or bends with the remover to remove:

O no! it is an ever-fixed mark

That looks on tempests and is never shaken"

I always believed love was eternal, that this love would last forever, that we would make it work through anything. I am the queen of adapting to difficult situations; why would this be any different? Because of my life experiences, I'm someone who doesn't waste time, who takes nothing for granted, who loves with all her heart, and who lets herself feel perhaps a bit too much. Today, I am feeling far too much: pain, confusion, anger, guilt. But most of all, I feel afraid to approach a life with my illness without someone to call when I don't want to burden my parents. I'm afraid to be sent off into the world alone to face the black curtain of my future.

I think back to the moment last summer when he held me in his arms and told me we were special, and everything I have ever believed in, everything I have ever been sure of disappears. I feel lost. Tomorrow he is leaving for school at the University of Southern California, and I'll be stuck here, fifteen minutes from my house at Stonehill College, a school that surely no one at USC will have heard of. A school so close to home, but so far from the guy I thought for sure I would spend forever with.

I walk through the front door of my house, catching a glimpse of my red eyes in the reflection of the storm door.

"He broke up with me," I cry to my mom and run upstairs to my bedroom.

She leaves me alone to cry. I look around my room, filled with memories of him: the teddy bear he built me at Build-a-Bear, sporting a pink bathrobe and named "Bear Naked," photos in frames, necklaces hanging on hooks, his sweatshirt draped across my desk chair, the scrapbook he made me for my birthday. I tuck it all on the top shelf of my closet and begin to pack for school.

Keeping busy is how I always deal with pain. My room looks spotless after a cry about my illness. Mom always knows I'm upset if my room is clean. When I'm happy and carefree, I can't be bothered to clean my room. I have life to appreciate! Soon it's 8 o'clock, and the late August sun begins to set. I lay down, too exhausted to cry any more, and drift off to sleep. I wake only when the door creaks open and my mom pokes her head in, checking on her heartbroken girl.

In a week, I'll be at Stonehill. Single. Left to face the world and my pesky lungs alone.

In the morning, the sun shines through the purple beads hanging in my window, and my eyes are swollen. Though I've never felt heartbreak before, something in me feels oddly familiar like all of the days I woke up in the morning to a day I had been looking forward to, but had to cancel because of cf. In a millisecond, when I open my eyes, the excitement fades away, when the IV in my arm comes into focus, or the syringes on my bedside table block access to the alarm clock, or the glow of the hospital hallway blinds me. Only this time, there's no physical reminder, just the tug of my heart drooping, sagging, and *drip drip* dripping into my stomach. I know this feeling. It's the frustration of your plans being ruined.

I was supposed to go into college in a relationship, a long distance one at that. I was supposed to marry my first love, probably right when we graduated, as to not waste any time. I was supposed to have him to call when I was upset. I was supposed to have a crutch. Cf causes so much uncertainty in my life, and he was my certainty. He was in those dreams I dreamt when I learned about the miracle drug. What would my future be without those dreams becoming a reality? This was a sure thing. Love *does not alter when it alteration finds.* Love doesn't ruin your fucking plans.

But something else in my life does. Cystic fi-fucking-brosis. And when it does, my parents taught me how to plan, think outside of the box, and get through it with a smile on my face. But this time it isn't as simple as that.

Don't Forget What's Down Cellar

Here's a sure thing: If *obstacle x* dictates your life, you are 100% guaranteed or your money back—to hate *obstacle x*.

That's why no one says thank you when someone breaks their heart, nor do we particularly like when our street doesn't get plowed here in the north. We humans are very quick to let *obstacle x* tell us there is nothing we can do, and then spend our time fuming about it.

But we humans are also very blessed with these big 'ol brains that have the ability to Figure. Shit. Out. If only we asked: So now what?

Since cf is so unpredictable, those little squatter bacteria sometimes invite a few too many friends to the party. I know when the party is getting out of hand when my trifecta of symptoms present themselves: (1) Too tired to get out of bed (2) coughing my brains out, and (3) inability to finish any meal and/or gagging with every bite. Usually, a period of denial, lasting anywhere from two days to one month, sets in. And depending on how long I deny the trifecta, the worse the news is when I finally learn that cf is kicking my butt, again. However, once that settles in, my mind always goes to one question: So now what?

Each time the doctor tells me that, yet again, it is time to be admitted into the hospital, my mind starts doing somersaults over the plans that will be missed, school assignments that will need re-routing, and most importantly, attitudes that will need adjusting. When cf throws a wrench in my plans, my mind goes right towards a resourcefulness that comes from my dad.

16

* * *

Growing up, we lived on a small, dead-end street. And like most kids, my best friend was the person who lived within the closest proximity, right next door. We had just entered second grade, and had the great fortune of experiencing a brand new jungle gym at school. And though the swings had always been our favorite playground adventure, the see-saw was our newest obsession.

I begged my parents for one, which of course they could not afford. They could have said, "No, you'll play with the one at school and be happy," but that's not how parents raised their millennial children now, is it?

Money was an obstacle, but Dad asked himself: So now what? He went to the back yard and grabbed a concrete block he had salvaged from our re-done patio. It was about 10-inches long, 6-inches high. Then, he dug through his scrap wood "down cellar," as us New Englanders call our basement, and re-appeared with a red 2x4. He balanced the long piece of wood on top of the concrete block and voilà, a see-saw. Even though it wobbled and creaked as it tried to round the sharp corner of the concrete block, we were so proud of our homemade see-saw, and quickly ran to tell our other neighborhood friends. The see-saw became the coolest toy in the neighborhood, even surpassing the prickly red berries that grew on our elderly neighbor's tree— perfect for chucking at kids of the opposite sex. Our see-saw was different, cool, and *red*.

When you have a problem to confront, look around and see what you already have to solve it.

As a kid, I wore my therapy vest every morning, and sometimes at night when I was feeling lousy. In the 90's, when the machine first came to the market, it was big and bulky—like most new technology in the 90's—and weighed what felt like a ton. Though it gave me the independence to do my airway clearance sans my dad to clap my chest, it tied me to the house. So when we wanted to go on vacation, I was out of luck or forced to get Chest PT from Dad, which after experiencing the convenience and comfort of the vest, I hated.

Until one day, Dad had an idea. The only thing holding us back from bringing my vest on vacation was the fact that it broke the average person's back in order to carry it to the car (airplanes were also out of the question). However, like most back breaking things, there are ways to transport them around without breaking your back. This is why most luggage has wheels. And this is why my dad took the wheels off of an old rolling chair in his shop down cellar and screwed them onto a few pieces of wood. *Voilà*, a dolly the perfect size for my vest. From the house, to the car, and into whatever house we were renting on Cape Cod, or into the mountains to ski, I could still keep myself healthy, and Dad was off the hook from doing chest PT on his vacation.

While Dad was able to solve our problems with his hammer, Mom was able to solve them by daring to ask. After all, the worse anyone could say was no.

In elementary school, I needed to take digestive enzymes every time I ate. While this meant going to the nurse every day at lunch time, I also needed to find her for every birthday party, Christmas celebration, and end of the year cupcakes. Some days there were sick kids needing her attention, and other days I was just last in the line of other pill-poppers. Which meant I missed out on most of the fun parties, had to leave recess early to grab the pills before lunch, and was always last in line for the cafeteria. But the school had rules. The nurse was the only one who could dispense medication, even though at home at the age of seven, I opened my own childproof containers, counted out the right amount, and swallowed them in one gulp, probably better than my own parents could.

All it took was a phone call to the school to convince them that the nurse was not the only one who could dispense medication, 7-year-old Lauren could, too. Surely my teachers could store the pill bottle in their locked desk, and hand it over to me to dispense on my own, like I did at home. I didn't miss another birthday celebration, was never late to lunch, and enjoyed recess right up until it ended.

When cf tried to get in my way, getting it to be less disruptive didn't have to be complicated. Creative solutions were often the most simple ones. And most of the time, the tools we needed were right in front of us: a concrete block and a 2x4, an old rolling chair, and a 7-year-old girl blessed with the ability to count as well as any school nurse.

During the times when what the doctor tells me is less than desirable, I look within to see what I already have to get through it. I have my experience—the hospital-street-smarts a kid like me learns from living it. I know what each visit to the hospital will entail: what nurse to ask for to place my PICC line (a device inserted in my arm to deliver antibiotics intravenously), to bring good lotion so the hospital air doesn't dry out my skin, and exactly what I need to pack to make it more enjoyable—a soft blanket, my own pillow, comfy clothes, a pad to draw and write, and, as I got older, a laptop to stay in touch with friends.

Thankfully, my dad's ingenuity taught me to be inventive when it came to managing the ways cf tried to break me. So that in times when I truly feel I can't live with the inconvenience, I have a pile in my basement of fixes. Sometimes it's a good book to get me through a long hospital stay. Other times it's a friend who I met in the hospital. Most often, it is knowing that anyone and everyone will bring me some sort of chocolate.

When going to the hospital meant I would miss out on much-cherished school time, I didn't let the fact that I wasn't in a classroom discourage me from keeping up with my peers. All it took was a plan, and asking my teachers if they'd keep me up to speed proactively. If I came to terms with the fact that I would be out of school sooner rather than later, I marched around to my various teachers and asked them for work for the next few weeks. They handed over lesson plans, print-outs, and books and sent me on my way, re-assuring me that they would help to catch me up and to just focus on getting better. I always kept up with the work and maintained my A average, and usually with a smile on my face.

Recently, I ran in a muddy, adventurous race, where not only did you have to run five miles, you had to jump over barriers, swim through mud pools, and climb 10-foot fences. Standing at five feet tall, I wondered how the heck I would climb the fence. Then, as I approached, I saw men on all fours, creating a stool of sorts. When you stood on their backs, you had just enough height to grab onto the hands of people waiting at the top. Without the men, it was an insurmountable fence, but with them, it was easy to climb right over and continue having a blast in the race.

People always comment that I am able to get through life and the challenges cf presents with a smile. It isn't that I have some unmatched strength that allows me to remain happy even though a disease is trying to kill me. It's because, when presented with an obstacle, I've learned to ask: So now what? And sometimes: Well why not? Because we as a family asked those questions, I didn't come to hate the obstacle.

You can't get over a 10-foot fence on your own, but you can stand on the backs of people and latch onto hands that will pull you up. I have an arsenal of tools that help me solve the problems cf causes. And when you're able to adjust your life using creative solutions that mean you can get through those barriers, of course you're going to smile.

Without resourcefulness and creative problem solving, your obstacles define you and your family, and dictate every single aspect of your lives. Dare to ask the question. Dare to look around and see what you have in front of and within you to make your obstacle, or your family's obstacle, or your kid's obstacle suck a little less. Maybe it isn't enough to make it go away, but it's enough to make you see it through fresh eyes. And when you do that, the hate subsides, the frustration eases, and life becomes a teensy bit more enjoyable.

The Dress

I'm in 7th grade, the age when your feet are too big for your body and your face and hair tend to be greasy. It's also the age when our school has its first semi-formal dance. Everyone gets dressed up, girls in sparkly dresses, boys in collared shirts and ties borrowed from their dads. Our first grown-up dance in our middle school's cafeteria.

It's what everyone talks about.

It's fall, and my lungs are tight and wheezy; I've been having a hard time breathing. Couple that with fevers due to the infection in my lungs and sinuses, and my mom starts to ask if it is time for a hospital visit. Her motherly Spidey senses go into high alert with every chest rattling cough.

Just a week before, I stood in a dressing room at the mall, Mom perched on a chair outside the door.

"How's it look, Honey?"

I tugged at the sides of the fabric, yearning for some semblance of a curve on my petite frame, willing the dress to give me a butt or boobs instead of falling down to my bony knees, following my stick figure frame.

"It's okay," I shrugged. "Not my favorite."

I pulled up the straps that had fallen down my shoulder. I opened the door and scrunched up my nose.

"Be right back!" Mom said after a quick glance at me.

It only took her a minute to grab the dress she was eyeing all along, but knew I wouldn't go for it with the way it looked on the rack. She knew that when she held it up for my inspection, that I would shrug and say, "Meh. Not my style." But she dared to have me try something different.

She returned with a red sparkly dress, in the smallest size they had.

"Just try it."

I rolled my eyes like pre-teens do and mumbled, "Fine."

Ripping off the offending dress, I took the sparkly dress off the hanger and slipped into it, the red sparkles reflecting off of the bright dressing room lights. I still had bony knees, thin shoulders, and was lacking in the boobs and butt department, but I was beautiful. I swung open the door, jumped out of the dressing room, and did a little boogie. This was it. We found cheap jewelry to match at Claire's, and I modeled the whole ensemble for my parents when we got home.

Now I sit in a doctor's office, breathing into a machine that will tell me how much my lungs have crapped out. The technician performing the test holds a straight face reading back the numbers, and by the lack of inflection in her voice, my heart sinks.

I have to get a cat-scan, because it's looking like this time the reason for my crappy lungs is my nose. Which means sinus surgery. This is a relatively simple surgery, usually, taking only a few hours under anesthesia.

"We'll want to get it done sooner rather than later, so plan for the sinus surgery in the next couple of weeks."

The dance is in fourteen days.

Let Yourself Be Mopey

Often, after giving a talk or writing a blog post fueled with positivity—looking on the bright side and covered in sunshine and rainbows—people will remark, often with tears in their eyes, "You are just so strong. It is so inspiring that you have been through so much and always have a smile on your face." Don't get me wrong, it is beyond flattering when people say this to me, and it's something I remind myself of when I don't feel so strong. But sometimes I feel like a phony.

When I'm feeling particularly humble, I'll say, "I've had to deal with this my whole life, and… really it's just something I've grown used to. My parents showed me early on that I can either let my challenges make me miserable, or I can let them shape me." In some ways, having a genetic illness my family and I have learned to deal with from an early age is a blessing. I can't remember a life where I didn't have this cough, where I didn't have to take medication every time I ate, or where I wasn't acquainted with cystic fibrosis.

What people mean when they say these things is that *they* don't think they would be able to deal with what I deal with, and still have a genuine enjoyment of life. When we think about the sacrifices people make, the ways in which our adversity casts a shadow on our expectations of what life is supposed to be, and we see people who continue to thrive despite the shadows, we are inspired. Inspiration stems from the admiration of someone doing something you never thought possible for yourself. That's why we cheer so loud for runners without legs, and people who fight wars, and cancer patients with bald heads. Because when you look inward, you don't see the strength that lies dormant, waiting for a challenge to wake it up.

Inside all of us lives the will to live—not just to live but to thrive, overcome, and adapt. Yet, this seems unthinkable to someone who has yet to be tested. Or perhaps you have been tested and feel a bit like I do—like the outward appearance of success isn't all that's there, that it took moments of doubt to allow the strength to reveal itself—and that you just did what you had to do at the time, given the circumstances, with what little resources you had. This resilience doesn't come easily. It takes a bunch of tears and let-downs to foster it.

Perhaps the single most difficult thing for me was the shift from, "this is a disease I have and will always have," to, "this is a disease that is not going away, and that is threatening to take my life." That shift occurred during one of the most challenging times: when I was a teenager.

It was an adjustment; something I wrestled with day in and day out, every single night before I went to bed. As a teenager, this sometimes meant I felt helpless, upset, and just plain angry at this disease that was killing other kids my age, that made me feel crummy, and that forced me to sit on the bench during field hockey season because I couldn't catch my breath long enough to chase down the other team. However, though those feelings came, they also went. I made a choice each time they snuck up on me. I'd let myself feel all the pain, cry all I needed to, and punch whatever non-breakable thing I could (usually a pillow). And then I'd make a plan, and do what I had to do to get through it.

Sitting in the car after getting the news that I needed sinus surgery and a hospital admission, I am now doing my usual routine of feeling all the pain. I'm counting on my fingers the fourteen days until the dance, calculating that they need to schedule the surgery either in the next two days, or in two weeks, a slim margin. I'm betting on trading in my red sparkly dress for a hospital gown. Sometimes, I can hold back the emotion until we get in the car, but most times the tears sneak out regardless. Usually, Mom picks up the car from the hospital valet, settles me into the back seat, and lets me cry.

"I know, sweetie," she'll say after I've let it all out.

Then she reminds me how quickly the hospital stay will go by.

"You'll be home before ya know it."

We talk about how much better I will feel, and at the end of her motivational speech, when I won't accept her re-assurances, I know she will smile and say, "Who loves ya, baby!?" Which has always made me smile, even when I want to roll my eyes. And I always respond back, "Mama loves me!"

That day in the car, after my doctor's appointment, we get through today's, "Who loves ya baby!?" But today, the smile doesn't come.

And like every other bad news day, Mom pulls into Friendly's just off the highway. I order my chicken fingers with a sundae for dessert, and usually, I'm laughing at her jokes by the end of the meal. But today those laughs don't come. Some days, on our way home from getting bad news, we stop by Old Navy to buy cozy pajamas for the stay. If it is going to suck, I may as well be both cozy and cute, in my frog printed satin PJ pants.

But I don't want to be cute in my frog printed satin PJ pants. I want to be cute in my red sparkly dress. So I let her drive past the stores.

Any other bad news day, when we get home she'll tell my Dad, who will come over and give me a hug, squeezing a little tighter than usual. I'll settle on the couch with my dog resting her chin on my lap and tell myself it will be alright, while my mom packs our bags, and calls work to make arrangements for being out. But not today. Today, I nuzzle my face into my dog and take a deep breath, burying my head in her soft ears, soaking them with tears. I just can't be resilient today.

Usually, by this point, we have all made an important, unspoken decision—we will take the next few weeks day by day, and do what we need to prepare. It is okay to be upset, but we have no choice but to get through it as a family. When the few weeks at the hospital are over, I know I will see the world through a new set of eyes. I always do. The sun will shine more brightly, my laugh will come more easily, and the struggle will make me appreciate the moments of ease. But I'm having a hard time believing all of this will happen this time.

Instead, all I can think about is coming back to school after spending time in the hospital, and seeing photos posted on the school bulletin board of my friends in their dresses, reminding me of what I'd missed.

The next day, my mom hangs up the cordless phone after speaking with the doctor.

"Lau, we're going to go in on September 19th, and you'll have sinus surgery some time that week."

I stare out the window and count the days in my head. Knowing that a hospital visit means at least a two week stay, I sigh.

"Ugh, so I *will* have to miss the dance," I say with tears welling up in my eyes.

I turn to hide them, walking up to my room. The stupid dress hangs on the door of my closet, where I will it to stay until the 8th grade semi-formal. Though maybe by then, I'll have boobs. I slip it off the hanger, and let it fall to the floor. It collapses to the floor almost as dramatically as I collapse on my bed.

Mom gives me an hour or so to sulk before she knocks on the door and peeks her head in. "I know, Lau. But think of how awesome your 8th grade dance will be."

"But it will be everyone else's second dance."

She considers this for a moment.

"You know what?" she says. "Usually by the second week you are feeling a lot better. Maybe you can do both."

"Both?" I say.

"Yeah, they let you leave the hospital to go to McDonalds across the street. Why not leave to go to your dance and come back after?" Mom says.

Why the hell not?

Why We Let the Faucet Leak

"Life isn't about waiting for the storm to pass, it's about learning to dance in the rain." -Vivian Greene

My dad is the type of man who doesn't throw anything away until it has fully served its purpose in life, even if its purpose isn't what was originally intended. Instead of, "if it ain't broke, don't fix it," he lives by the motto, "if it still works, regardless of its inconvenience, don't replace it, duct tape it, and work it until it is truly dead... and then use it for something else."

So that's why, growing up, I never thought it odd that the toilet ran until you jiggled the handle ever so slightly. Or that in order to get the timer to work on the oven, you had to pinch it with a pair of needle nose pliers because the knob had fallen off. Or that to turn on the gas burners on the stove you had to borrow the one remaining knob to light all four. I never thought it was entirely troublesome that, if you wanted to see while going down the basement stairs, you had to twist the light bulb on the wall because the pull-string had fallen off long ago. And if you forgot to turn it off before it got too hot, I never thought twice as I went into the kitchen to find an oven mitt to protect my hand.

I never dared to question the fact that the upstairs bathroom sink only ran hot water, so you had better wash your hands quickly before it turned scalding hot. And the pile of random materials that were stacked in the basement, and in the backyard, just blended into the backdrop of the decor. Because those egg cartons became the body of the mouse-trap car I had to make in elementary school. The old 5-gallon buckets in the basement became a squirrel defense system—turned upside down, drilled into, and placed halfway up the bird feeder so those gray pests would stop stealing the robins' food. And things that hadn't yet found another purpose soon revealed them unintentionally: like when the above-ground pool Dad had set up—that used to be in his own backyard in the 70's—finally caved in. Underneath the 6-foot high pool deck, leaning against the pool wall, were random pieces of scrap metal and wood. Dad proudly nudged my shoulder and said, "and if it wasn't for your old swing-set I had piled up under the pool-deck, our backyard would have been covered in water."

Merely tolerating annoyances was putting it lightly. As I got older, moved into my own apartment, and had my own household problems to fix (or to beg my landlord to fix), I lost all patience for the small accommodations we made growing up.

One day, I sit in the living room with my parents and brother as they, "wait for the TV to turn on." It takes about 20 minutes of the TV automatically turning on and off… and on and off, all the while making loud screeching noises, as if it was using everything in its power to allow us to watch the evening news. I whip my head back and forth as my mom patiently scrolls through Facebook on her laptop, my dad reads his book, and my brother texts his friends. Even the dog has grown used to this. Which was surprising, considering every time my brothers and dad either cheered or yelled obscenities at the Red Sox, Patriots, or Celtics, the dog's tail went between her legs. But as the TV wails, she lays on my mom's feet, as if it were October and the Red Sox had safely not made it to the playoffs.

At this point, I laugh. And I can't stop. How ridiculous it is that my family thinks nothing of this TV howling at them, practically screaming that it has reached the end of its very long life, a 50-inch plasma screen that was probably the first of its kind?

"You do this EVERY DAY?!" I gasp, exasperated, astonished. "Why don't you just get a new TV?!"

My dad, realizing the ridiculousness of it all, defends his TV that is not 100% broken yet.

"Whatever! It works in the end—see?!"

He points to the screen, in perfect High Definition. I shake my head and can only laugh. It's cute, the way my dad, and by effect the rest of the household, simply adjusts to these little annoyances and inconveniences. And if watching TV means sitting through 20 minutes of painful loud noises, then so be it. At least they have a TV that works in the end.

That night, I tell the story to my husband.

"Now I know where you get it from," he says.

"What do you mean?" I proclaim.

"See that shoe over there? It's been in the middle of the kitchen floor for two weeks now. And I watch you every morning just step right over it, as if it isn't there."

At this, I laugh. Don't we all have a moment in our existence where we realize that the things our parents do that annoy the hell out of us, begin to manifest themselves in our own lives?

As we go to bed, I think back to the blaring TV, and my kitchen shoe. How simple it would be to just get a new TV, or put away the freaking shoe. But the way my dad and I function has a lot to do with the inconveniences we've learned to deal with in our everyday life. Perhaps I have become so accustomed to the fact that cf will be there, still allowing my body to work, regardless of its inconvenience, that I choose to duct tape it, and continue to live until it has done all the damage it is going to do. And like that blaring TV, cf with all of its pain, and annoyance, and inconvenience, has just become something I am used to, step over, and live life around. At least, through it all, my body still works to get to where it needs to be. And when it doesn't, I find a 5-gallon bucket to get me through in the meantime—keeping the squirrels out of my spirit so that the birds with their songs could get the seeds.

The times when I've learned the most about my own ability to tolerate inconveniences, are the times when we as a family refuse to let the blaring TV bother us, and continue on with life as usual despite it.

As a parent, it is up to you to see what you have within you to get through life despite the issues your child's illness or disability presents, to dance in the rain. What rituals have you found work? What decisions have you made despite the glaring elephant in the room? If you don't find it within yourself to continue to live, despite every annoyance and barrier your child's disease presents, your child's disease takes control. You take the reigns back when you begin to make decisions despite the barriers. What can you do to be in control?

The One Thing Your Kid Needs
When the World is Unfair

It's my junior year of high school, and I am being admitted to the hospital for two weeks. Like every time I've gone to the hospital since the first grade, I talk to my teachers and arrange for homework while away. They hurriedly comply, my French teacher assigning pages in our workbook, and even letting me borrow tapes to listen to. My English teacher presents me with the next novel we are going to read, along with the corresponding assignments, and my history teacher prints out supplemental material ahead of time, neatly arranging it in a packet.

And then I get to my math teacher. He is brilliant, and has a way of teaching that is beyond the norm. No textbooks, no worksheets. Just a man and his chalk board, with problems written down at the end of each class. I ask him for some work.

"Well," he says, "I don't really have a book… so I'll just catch you up when you get back."

And off I go, my backpack full of papers and books for my two-week absence.

Where my first hospital visits were met with visitors, presents, and things to do, this visit is different. The hospital has implemented new guidelines that mean people with cf can't leave their rooms, for fear of cross-infection. Since I'm older, too, I don't want my parents staying with me every night, so I shoo them away, happy to spend the nights alone.

And though my normal visitors never fail to show, it seems more and more people are too busy to stop by. Plans are made and never followed through, and in the new world of social media, a post on your wall is enough to make people feel they have done their good deed for the day. So the nights are lonely, as these visits have become so commonplace for me by now.

I keep busy with my school work, relieved that I am able to push off math until I return, and practice my French, read my novel, and write a fine history paper.

Soon enough, I return to school and sit in my math class. Boy, am I behind. My teacher breezes through derivatives, which swirl around my head like a tornado. Typically the one to raise my hand, to always know the answer, and to wait for my classmates to catch up, now I am the one who is confused.

I doodle on my paper as I try to understand this new math function, and bite my lip.

After school, I waltz into the class and sit down. I ask my teacher to start from the beginning, and he does, drawing out some equations on a scrap piece of paper. I ask questions, as I would in class.

"You know," he remarks. "Just because you were in the hospital isn't an excuse not to know this stuff."

I fume, feeling the prick of tears behind my eyes, and quickly breathe in to try and quell them. Realizing he has just said something extremely offensive, he tries to laugh it off. I breathe in and try forcing a smile.

"But you said you would catch me up..."

He calls loudly for the teacher next door, "Can you teach her this?"

I huff and smile at her, a smile so big it would hide any of the alarm in my eyes.

She reluctantly takes me into her room and we sit down, looking at the notes scribbled on the paper. Embarrassed, ashamed, and completely pissed off, I take a breath and try to hide it, getting on with my questions as quickly as I can. I just want to get out of here.

Finally, the lesson is over and I gather my notebook, stuff it in my bag, and walk hurriedly to my car in the back parking lot. I whip open the door, jam my car key into the ignition, and speed home, breathing heavily, the tears coming quickly.

I storm into the house to my parents in the kitchen.

"He refused to teach it to me! He told me I can't use being in the hospital as an excuse!"

I slump down into a chair in the dining room, and hold my hands to my eyes.

"Mom, you remember, right?! He told me he would catch me up!"

For someone so rigid in her schooling, who spent every day in the hospital trying to keep up the pace, I couldn't believe he had said I was using it as an excuse. I would never.

My mom rushes over and rubs my arm, while my dad grabs something from the counter, flipping through a stack of books and junk mail.

"Honey, that isn't right!" she says.

"I hate him!" I continue venting. "I can't believe him!"

Dad comes to sit down with something he had grabbed.

Soon I am hysterical, and I see the concern building up in Mom's face.

She looks up and says, "John, what are you doing?"

My even-tempered, brush-it-off-your-shoulder father is flipping through a book. The phone book. Scanning his finger down the page.

"Found it," he smirks.

"John, no! No you are not going to his house. Are you crazy?!"

Then, he loses it.

"How the hell could he say that? To Lauren of all people!"

I start laughing, a huge belly laugh, at the thought of my dad marching over to the teacher's house. Who knows what he thought would happen. A real brawl? A proper duel? He starts laughing too, exasperated at how to solve this problem for his princess.

"Dad, I love your commitment, but you don't have to go over there."

Sometimes we don't need a solution. We just need someone to show us it's okay to be upset when the world is unjust. We just need someone to remind us we are loved despite it. And when your kid is living with a life-threatening illness, sometimes that's all you can offer them—even when you wish you could give them the world, take away all their pain, and see a smile on their face.

What my dad didn't know, in that moment, is that I knew, without a doubt, that he loved me, unconditionally. The kind of love where he would fight for me, where he understood exactly how I was feeling. And that love validated all of my emotions, and reassured me that I wasn't in this alone. His furious phone book flipping was all I needed to know that I had a man by my side who loved his little girl, and would stop at nothing to see me smiling again.

I also knew that regardless of what that teacher said to me, cf was never used as an excuse in that way. My parents knew it, and so did I. The only thing we used cf as an excuse for was to live fiercely, passionately, and to take in every single moment.

That's love, right there. Throughout my life, all I have ever needed to know is that I'm not in this alone. When life isn't fair and people try to let cf define me, I have my parents to go through it with me, to get just as furious, and just as upset at how unfair it all is, but to also make me laugh and bring me back to reality. Love is hugging someone when they're upset, telling them it will be okay. Sometimes the biggest acts of love are when you go through the tough emotions with your kid; it reminds them that what they're feeling is real, and that they aren't alone.

What no one tells you when have a child with a chronic illness is that life is going to be unfair. People are going to be mean, they're going to hurt your feelings, they'll try to put barriers on you where there shouldn't be any, and they'll say things that make you want to march over to their house and tell them what is up. A lot of us go through life thinking everyone should just *be* better, that it isn't up to us to tell that teacher they shouldn't tell your teen with cf, who was freshly discharged from the hospital, that she is using her life-threatening illness as an excuse not to do her calculus homework. We think it isn't our responsibility to educate the world about why that isn't fair. The world should just know.

Well, in some ways, it is our responsibility to be advocates. The world won't know until we tell them, and sometimes you need to sit the person down and explain to them, calmly and kindly, why what they said was hurtful, or how they misunderstood your situation. But what you learn when you are dealing with a chronic illness, or disability in your family, is to pick your battles. When every day seems like a battle in and of itself, you cannot be expected to confront every injustice that presents itself. Given the immense amount of inequity in the world, we simply cannot fight every little unfair word, action, and inaction. We would live a hate-filled life if we did that, and would make more enemies than friends. What we need is compassionate understanding, very thick skin, and to know when the situation warrants some schooling in the life of a sick kid. What your kid needs when it happens to them is for you to simply love them. When you love them, the rest comes naturally.

Be A Mama Bear

You would think that since my Mom is a nurse, she would be over-protective. She knows every germ, every sickness, knows how to recognize the beginnings of serious illnesses, and sees the ultimate end they cause. To say she doesn't worry would be a lie, but she has a keen understanding of the importance of a life well lived over a life that is safe, free from harm, or devoid of the many lessons left to learn.

My mom could arrange for me to sit out in gym class. She could home school me, to keep me from the germs my classmates inevitably bring to the playground, the classroom, and the school bathrooms. Sanitization could have been my mother's middle name, ensuring no bacteria escaped the clutches of her disinfectant. She could have made it her mission to kill every microbe, every bacterium, every virus. But, she sees the happiness on my face when I splash around a public hot tub with my cousins in New Hampshire, she is thankful for the friends I've made in school who remind me to take my pills at lunch, and she feels the warmth of love on vacations, when the family snuggles on the beach at sunset, knowing full well that I will fall asleep on the car ride home and won't have time to do my treatments. She made a decision early on that life in a bubble wasn't a life at all.

Are some of the decisions she makes risky? Of course. But perfection means that I miss out on too much, and if my life is going to be short, that is an even greater risk she isn't willing to take.

Obviously, my health is a number one priority. But when that priority keeps butting heads with me getting to experience life, with all of its opportunities and fleeting moments, she chooses life. Every single time.

And so, here I am in 7ᵗʰ grade, lanky and growing into my body, preoccupied with boys, school gossip, and reading Seventeen magazine, sitting at the dinner table the day after Mom and I decided I am going to that dance.

"The school rule is if you are absent the day of a dance, you aren't allowed to go," I declare.

When the Vice Principal's voice came over the intercom to remind us about the rules of the dance, my heart sunk for the second time that week.

"No exceptions," she ended, after listing off a barrage of rules related to dress codes, the proper distance between dancing couples, and how only students present the day of the dance could attend.

I'm pouting at the dinner table, unwilling to accept the heavy hand our Vice Principal tried to dole out on the morning announcements.

My mom is never one to fight my battles for me. But when it comes to cf, her mama bear instincts come out; she claws her way through the conversation until a person understands why "punishing" her daughter for being sick is so unjust. She is a rule follower, and she knows when her kid is in the wrong. Never one to step on others' toes, or cause too much controversy, she usually lets things roll off her shoulders. But when people try to impose restrictions on me because of my cf she roars, she advocates, and she lets them into our world until they understand.

I kneel beside the kitchen table and crack the window so I can hear her outside on the cordless phone. She politely asks for the Vice Principal by name, and calmly explains her reason for calling. I see her shadow move in front of the window, waiting through the silence on the line, breathing a sharp breath in through her nose.

After explaining that her daughter will be in the hospital the day of the dance, I guess the Vice Principal says something like, "I'm sorry, but those are the rules," because I hear the *shing* of her claws appearing.

"You know," she pushes on, "my husband and I have always tried to give Lauren the best life possible, and refused to let cf get in the way of that. So

37

I'd really appreciate it if you reconsidered your rules right now."

Her voice shakes the slightest bit at, "right now," and I feel the tension in her teeth at each syllable. It sounds like the Vice Principal's tone is softening a bit, with only a few words mumbled on the line. I hold my breath. The next words can't come soon enough.

"Thank you. Yes, yes, I understand. Thank you. She'll be thrilled."

Crouching back down, I fist pump under the table and start thinking about my sparkly red dress under my 7th grade crush's hands. One foot away, of course.

Then I bite my lip because for the first time, in that moment, I choke up for reasons that are unusual to my pre-teen self. It isn't because I'm upset about the rules, or embarrassed that my mom is arguing with the woman who controlled the lunch room with various hand explosions (when we had something to celebrate we all had to make fireworks with our hands, sssssssing the wick until it exploded with a clap!). No, in this moment, I feel loved. But for the love of all things holy, I can't let my mom know that. How uncool.

So I scurry up from under the table and rush to the living room to grab the remote, pretending to adjust the volume of whatever is playing on MTV, and ask her how it went.

"You're goin' to the dance!" she shrieks. "Who loves ya, baby!?"

I smile, letting on the slightest bit how pleased I am.

"Mama loves me…"

And like we do each time I finally let the inevitability of the hospital sink in, we make a plan. I'll have the surgery on Monday, we will leave the hospital on Friday so that I can go get ready with my friends, I'll attend the dance with Mom nearby in her car, and we'll get back to the hospital in time for my night-time antibiotic infusion.

"We'll make it an adventure!" Mom says.

Make it an Adventure

I'm 7 years old, the therapy vest has just been released by HillRom, and the doctor brings it in for me to try during my first hospital stay. She adjusts the buckles on the front of the black vinyl vest, plugs the long plastic tubes into the holes on the machine, and hands me the black rubber pedal I will sit on to turn it on. I watch her fiddle with the settings, push the pedal in my hands, and soon the vest whirrs to life. My mom, her eyes alight, asks how it feels.

"I-I-I-I-t f-e-e-l-s f-u-n-n-n-y!" my voice shakes with the speed of the vest.

The doctor shows us how to use it, how I will stop and take deep breaths while holding down the button on the highest setting after the timer *dings*. As soon as she leaves we go to work on this new adventure.

"Sing Twinkle Twinkle Little Star!" Mom pleads.

"U-p a-bove the world s-o h-i-i-i-igh," I draw out the words to let my voice shake, turning it high pitched and giggling as I go. We go on like this until I have sung every song we can think of, including Britney Spears latest single, "Baby One More Time."

The doctor, hearing the commotion, comes back in with narrowed eyes.

"That's a $10,000 toy you're playing with!"

We muffle our giggles in our hands and listen to her heels click down the hall. An instant later, I try out my ABCs, continuing the adventure with my expensive new toy.

* * *

Judging by the quiet hum of the fluorescent lights in favor of kid's voices, it's past all of our bedtimes at Children's Hospital. In the entertainment center, I drop a few of my mom's quarters in the juke box and pick one of my favorites: "Build Me Up Buttercup." My mom grabs my hands and we boogie on the foot-high wooden stage. Dad does a classic Dad Move, stepping from side to side and pointing his fingers at me. Twirling and laughing, I jump up and down in my Sleeping Beauty nightgown, watching the fabric rise and fall with gravity.

We get back to my room past visiting hours, and then sneak out to the kitchen to grab some ice cream cups from the freezer. Creeping down the quiet hallway in my socks with the little grips on the bottom makes me smirk slyly, my mom tiptoeing beside me and miming paws with her hands. She hums the *Pink Panther* theme song, "daa-dum, daa-dum, da-dum da-dum-da-dum," like she did the time we raided the refrigerator on my Girl Scout trip to the Children's Museum.

* * *

Make it an adventure, so that the sucky stuff can suck less.

When I think back to the hospital, I don't particularly remember the scary nights in bed, the roommates who weren't always pleasant, or the tears that came with each needle prick. What I remember are the adventures.

Friends and cousins come to visit, and it is another adventure. Mom tells them to hop up on the bed. We have hospital bed rides, pressing the buttons and moving the bed up high, tilting it as we sit on either end, and holding on tight as we move it back down, giggling at the new experience.

My favorite adventure happened one night after I had checked into the hospital. My mom had bought me slippers with pink kitties on them that meowed every time I stomped my feet. As we waited in the hallway for an X-ray, my mom made me do things to make my kitty feet meow: jump off a chair, march up and down the hallway, kick my legs up like the Rockettes. An X-ray tech finally came out, looked up at the ceiling, and then down the hall at me jumping off chairs in my kitty slippers.

"Oh my goodness! We were just freaking out because we thought there was a cat loose in the ceiling!"

Our trip down to the X-ray department late that night went from something new and scary, to something fun and exciting! I got to waltz around the hospital in my new kitty slippers, making them meow for all to hear, and even tricking the X-ray techs!

We make everything an adventure when it comes to my cf. Each hospital visit, I looked forward to taking a trip to the gift shop and picking out a new toy. In the winter, we would go to the hospital and then take the subway to downtown Boston to see the Enchanted Village Christmas display, filled with animated figures in cute Christmas scenes. It was exciting to walk down Longwood Ave., where the hospital was, run across the street, and catch the T just in time to head downtown.

For me, the adventure was in the unknown. I hadn't quite worked out whether this place was good or bad. I heard kids crying in the hallways, and I saw the solemn looks on their parents' faces. But I also heard laughter more than cries, and felt the warmth of the nurses, doctors, and hospital clowns, who stopped by with things like fart machines and animal balloons. Each day was an opportunity to learn the ropes of hospital life, but it was also filled with a lot of fear, a sprinkle of uncertainty, and a dab of hesitancy.

If throughout that fear and uncertainty I could make the nurses think a kitten was stuck in the rafters, and I could look forward to seeing the moving figurines at the Enchanted Village, or I could dance on a stage when everyone was sleeping, then that fear and uncertainty wasn't so bothersome. And when I got older, it meant that despite the fear of what others thought about my very personal health struggles, I could make them laugh with a foray into the world of my treatments.

Don't get me wrong, the fear sits there, always, tucked right next to the hope, the positivity, and the bad jokes—from the day I first slept in that hospital to the nights lying in bed as an adult wondering what surprises my health will give me tomorrow. Growing up, though, I learned to position the fear right next to the adventures, turning it into excitement—something else that makes my heart thump and wonder what's next. The thing is, with adventure, you get to find out what's in that hospital kitchen, what songs live inside that juke-box, and what is possible in the face of a life-threatening illness. If only for a minute, adventure overshadows fear, casting it into the dark, a mountain blocking the sun until it shifts to the west.

As a parent, you have the power to turn the ordinary into the extraordinary. When you and your child enter a world filled with uncertainty, it is the perfect time to say, "Let's make it an adventure." Then the fear becomes excitement, and you can explore this unchartered territory together, like Pink Panthers in the night, rather than fearfully navigating the forest without a flashlight.

A Little Pressure

So, off we go to the hospital, with the expectation that in one week's time, I will feel well enough to escape the hospital and dance away with my 7th grade boyfriend.

But cf, as it usually does, has other plans. The sinus surgery went swimmingly. None of the scary side effects the doctors are required to list off right before they drug you have happened, so from past experience, I know this means a quick recovery. On the third day, I lightly blow my nose, only to find a little bit of blood. This is normal, as the passageways in my nose begin to heal and get used to the fact that they aren't clogged with mucus. I throw away the tissue, wash my hands, and resume the book I was reading.

Soon, a doctor enters and says, "Oh here, let me grab you a tissue."

What? I grab the tissue, touch it to my nose, and find enough blood to saturate the tissue through. The bleeding hadn't stopped. And it doesn't stop, for six whole hours.

Mom had gone home that morning, so I call to tell her about the blood situation. While sitting at a hair appointment, the dye still in her hair, she tells me it's going to be okay. After she hangs up, she motions to her hairdresser.

"Wash this out of my hair right now! I gotta go!"

She drives to the hospital, hair still wet, and walks in just as the doctors are explaining their Plan A. Do you know what doctors do when you have a nose bleed that won't stop? Well… they do the same thing a female does when she has a uterus that bleeds once a month. They put a tampon in it.

Up until this point, tampons were still far too scary for me to use. So it was a bit amusing that the first time I was using one it was being shoved into the exact opposite side of my body. Although they call it "packing," I know better than to trust that name.

They continue to explain that it will hopefully put pressure on wherever the blood is coming from, while also absorbing it to make me a little more comfortable. But putting it in was going to cause, "some pressure." "Pressure," is a word doctors use when it will feel slightly uncomfortable, without making you wince.

This was not pressure. They begin, and I hold my mom's hand as they literally lube it up with Vaseline and start to insert it into my nose. I wonder how this long piece of dense cotton, the length of a somewhat sharpened pencil, is going fit into my nose—more the length of a hand-held eraser.

I feel the tampon enter what seems to be my brain, stretching and filling my already sore, bleeding nose. On a scale of happy face to very sad face, this is a VERY, VERY SAD FACE. Emojis aren't really a thing yet, but if I had one to use it would be the guy crying in anguish, the one you use when you realize you and your friend's schedules don't line up to hang out.

I scream. And I NEVER scream with pain. It's loud, and echoes down the hallways, as my body wrings itself out, contorting in ways I never knew it could. And then, it's over. I vaguely hear them telling me I can breathe now, and feel my heart rate coming down.

About an hour later, the doctors realize that Plan A has not gone as planned. The doctor shines a light in my mouth and tells me that blood is still trickling down my throat. The doctors take my mom out into the hallway. A few minutes later she comes back in to explain Plan B.

"So, they are going to have to cauterize inside your nose in order to stop the bleeding.

What have you had to eat today?"

I tick off my meals.

"Okay," she says. "Well, they'll give you anesthesia anyways, but they're going to have to suck out the food from your belly."

The words click in my head. Anesthesia means I am going in for surgery. It is 3:00pm; the semi-formal is at 8:00pm. The doctors come in and explain that it will only take about 20 minutes, and that I'll be awake by 5:00pm.

"Okay, perfect. So I'll be able to make it to the semi-formal then."

"Lauren, even though this is quick… you are still going in for surgery. I wouldn't plan on going to the dance tonight."

Duh. How silly of me to think I could be two hours post-op and still attend the dance. My mom briskly tucks the red sparkly dress into my closet while I change into a starched hospital gown and remove my jewelry.

"Mom, you gotta talk to them. I can make it! I feel fine other than the fact that I have a tampon up my nose."

"We'll see," she says.

And I am wheeled in my hospital bed down to surgery.

How to Make Risky Decisions

The adventures I look back on as a kid were fun and exhilarating, but only because I knew no real harm would come from "stealing" ice cream from the hospital refrigerators. The real adventures, the ones that truly test a sick kid, are filled with risk, what-if's, and uncertainty. They are the times when you wonder, "should we *really* be doing this?"

Life with any illness, but especially a chronic, unpredictable one like cf, is uncertain, surprising, and unexpected. One day your family is enjoying a vacation on the beach, or planning for your child's graduation, or decorating for Christmas, and the next your kid's symptoms have flared up and derailed your plans. The adventure lies in the decisions you make in that moment. You need to decide (1) whether life can still go on, (2) whether embarking on the adventure is worth the risk, and regardless of the choice (3) to look through a new lens.

Can life still go on?

Sometimes, you *do* have to drop everything and focus on your sick kid's health. That's hard, but it's also okay. The decision you make here has to do with what you choose to see. One of my favorite college professors had us do an activity during our, "Creative Process," class. He stood at the front of our class during the first week of the semester and instructed us to walk from our classroom to the library.

"On your way and once you're in the library, look around and try to remember everything you see that's brown."

The girl in the class who you could tell was going to be the one who asked too many questions raised her hand.

"Can we take our notebooks?"

"No," he said, "Just try to remember."

I quickly went to work noticing the trees, the bookcases, the soil in the planters, the books themselves. I saw brown in the paintings hanging on the walls, on people's boots, their jackets, and the doors. Finally, when fifteen minutes was up, he told us to walk back to class. After everyone had sat down, he turned to us.

"Now," he said, "tell me everything you saw that was red."

A room filled with overachievers, desperate to please the teacher on our first day, sat in stunned silence. The girl who asked about the notebook raised her hand.

"I think I saw someone wearing a red sweater?" she offered.

Then, our Professor named all the red things on the way from the classroom to the library. Tulips planted on the walk ways, the red brick path, the apples by the coffee stand, the beautiful painting on the stairwell.

"If you walk around the world wearing shit colored glasses, all you're going to see is shit," he said.

One New Years Eve, I was dealing with a rough lung infection, and had to be home with a PICC line to receive antibiotics. My friends were having a New Years Eve party, and we had to decide whether it was worth the risk to go. Faced with 102 degree fevers and weakness throughout my body, I knew I couldn't make it to midnight, let alone to ten o'clock. It wasn't worth it to wear my body out when New Years happens every year.

So I didn't get to go be with my friends when the ball dropped, like I looked forward to every year. But rather than mope around and pretend it wasn't a major holiday, we took off our shit colored glasses, and made the most of it. Dad made my favorite dinner, and Mom set up a table next to the fireplace to make it a little more special. We talked about how relaxing it was to be with family, about how I may be sick but at least we still had a toasty fire to warm our toes by—and we still laughed while playing games together by the light of the fire. I didn't make it to midnight, but I still wore a gold paper New Years hat, and glasses where the zeros in the year were eye holes. Did I miss my typical New Years Eve? Of course. But when life as usual cannot continue due to sickness, we decide to reframe our expectations, look around and notice what we do have, and be thankful for it.

Is it worth the risk?

Sometimes, the calculated risk is such that life can still go on. And the answer to the question, "should we really be doing this?" is a resounding, "yes," if it means a quality life for your kid *and* they still get the care they need. The internet is filled with viral moments of brides getting married in their hospital beds, girls who are bald from chemotherapy rocking it at their proms, and kids receiving millions of cards when they spend their holidays in the hospital. One person with cf, upon hearing she needed IV antibiotics, asked her doctors if she could go surf in Hawaii instead, because she thought that would make her lungs feel better. And surf in Hawaii she did!

Humans have the ability to allow life to go on, though the circumstances may be untraditional—and everyone eats it up when they do. But still, too many people decide to put it off, save it for another day, or cancel it entirely when illness rears its ugly head. Adventures are adventures because we are up against something that seems impossible, and when we don't allow life to go on, we let our barriers keep making life impossible.

As a senior in high school, my brother Danny decided he wanted to be a nurse like my mom. His college essay was all about how he looked up to his little sister, even though its typically the other way around. The day his acceptance letter came from The University of New Hampshire's nursing program, he picked me up and carried me on his back all the way up our dead-end street.

Four years later, when Danny was graduating from college in New Hampshire two hours away, and I was dealing with a serious fever from strong antibiotics, we calculated the risk. I needed my rest, but I also was so looking forward to seeing my big brother get his degree in nursing. Which was more important? Or could we make both happen?

In the end, we decided we could make it work. We packed up my IV pole. And even though I slept in the back of the car and spent the rest of the day in a hotel bed, I got to wake up and see him walk across the stage, something he was committed to do after watching me grow up sick. I watched as his professor gave him his nursing pin, and seeing him fist pump, I imagined all the little kids he would take care of, and how they'd remember him just like I remembered my nurses.

One year, I was sick during the holidays yet again. I spent the days leading up to Christmas with carolers singing outside my hospital door, meeting Boston sports players in Santa hats, and accepting teddy bear gifts dropped off by volunteers.

I was excited that I got to go home the day before Christmas Eve, even though I still had my PICC line and needed IV antibiotics eight times a day. That night, we had tickets to *A Christmas Story*, a play in Boston. I jumped in the back seat of the car to head home and asked my mom what time we needed to leave for the play.

"Oh, gosh, I just figured we wouldn't go, Lau," she said.

"Why the hell not?!" I pushed. "There's no reason I can't infuse my meds there, plus I have these portable medicine balls now."

"Are you sure you feel up to it?"

"Yes! We are going."

Rather than stay home to get set up with the homecare agency, we called the nurse and told her she'd have to wait until tomorrow. My parents and I went to the play, with me infusing medications at the restaurant before, a syringe in my lap to flush through the medication when it was done. I laughed along with, "You'll shoot your eye out kid," and all the classic moments I loved in the movie, especially Ralphie's pink bunny suit.

When I was getting ready to graduate from college, I saw a photo of Yosemite National Park online and told my parents I wanted to go. They carefully planned the trip, and soon after graduation we boarded a plane and landed in San Francisco. After picking up our rental mini-van, we drove six hours to the National Park.

It was hard to breathe in the high altitude. It felt like weights were pulling down the lobes in my lungs, but I was determined to climb the trail I picked out in the guide book—the Four Mile Trail, famous for offering a view of every awe-inspiring scene in the park: Half Dome, El Capitan, and Yosemite Falls.

I had never gone on a hike this long, let alone at 8,000 feet. But I decided I could make it up the mountain, even if it was slowly, and take the car down from the top. My boyfriend and I climbed up the steep switchbacks, stopping at every corner so I could catch my breath. Each time I stopped, I turned to look at the stunning scenery. The other mountains were actually purple, the sky was bluer than I'd ever seen, and I was in awe of the sheer size of everything: the mountains, the waterfalls, the cliffs.

Planning out the hike with the guidebook, I didn't expect it to take nearly the entire day, but rather than moan about my unmet expectations, I decided to look for the positives. The slow, steady pace allowed me to take in all the beauty, and every turn of the switchback I reminded myself how lucky I was to be there, regardless of how difficult it was. When we got to the top, the view was worth every break, every cough, and every time I thought I should just give up and walk down.

Look through a new lens

How great it is to be able to say, "Yes, we faced this barrier, and we *still* experienced all that life had to offer." The times in my life when my family and I made these decisions were even *more* meaningful than the status quo. When I think back to those moments, I see how impossible they seemed at the time, but I love that I can say, "I did it, anyway." You see those ordinary moments through a new lens when you decide to do them despite the barriers illness creates. They become magnified: more meaningful, and more memorable. And it all starts with a choice. Can life still go on? Is this worth it? How can you use your barriers to see your situation in a new light?

The Only Song You Need
to Combat Judgement

If you were sitting next to us after I begged my mom to let me go to the dance, you would have rolled your eyes. How cute and silly of this young girl to think she is going to come out of surgery, put on a dress, and go dancing, still groggy from the anesthesia.

But, we *are* talking about people who refuse to let the fact that there's no switch on the light bulb to keep them from seeing, as long as they had oven mitts to screw in the bulb. And that meant we also happen to be people who refuse to let the fact that I was going to be a bit drowsy (but otherwise blood free) prevent me from attending my first semi-formal dance.

An hour later I'm back in my room, fully awake. I look at my mom again. "Just ask."

And ask she does. She convinces them that everything will be fine.

"I'm a recovery room nurse. I'll stay in the building if anything comes up."

"Fine," they say. "But only because you're a nurse. And she has to be back by midnight for her antibiotic infusion."

"Hear that, Lau! If you're not back by midnight you're gonna turn into a pumpkin!"

Although we were supposed to leave and get ready with my friends, time doesn't allow for that. I have 20 minutes to get ready, and flummoxed, I try to curl my hair with my barely bendable arm, my PICC line wrapped in a red bandage around my elbow to match my dress. When it comes out flat and uneven, Mom helps me to twist it back into a ponytail, framing the front of my face with two rhinestone hair clips.

Once she's done fixing my hair, I close the bathroom door, and look into my eyes in the mirror, my skin looking translucent under the buzzing fluorescent lights framing the mirror. I see the sparkly eyeshadow on my eyelids, hiding their purple tint, the thin red spaghetti straps, safety pinned in the back to keep them from falling off my bony shoulders. I practice holding my arms behind my back to hide the bright red bandage covering my IV for pictures. What will everyone say? "Just give 'em something to talk about," I sing in my head.

* * *

Just a year before, I sat in this same hospital room, IMing with Hannah from school while I waited for Mom and Dad to come back from their run home to make me a fresh cooked dinner, my favorite: steak teriyaki. Hannah and I chatted about the hospital and how gross the food was, and I asked her what I was missing at school.

"Well, umm, Jimmy is spreading rumors that you're in the hospital for, well… slitting your wrists."

I laughed out loud, nervously.

"LOL what? Who told him that?"

"Idk u no Jimmy, he makes stuff up. But I told people that wasn't true, don't worry." "Well, doctas here. TTYL."

The doctor came in to check my breathing, and I inhaled and exhaled shaky breaths, trying hard not to let what Hannah said bother me. I counted my breaths and tried to focus on the cues the doctor was giving me, and must have done a pretty good job because he didn't notice anything was off.

"Mom and Dad coming in soon?"

"Yeah, they'll be here soon…"

"Well, enjoy your night!"

A few minutes later in walked Mom and Dad. Mom looked at me a second longer, her Spidey senses telling her something was up when I forced a smile and looked out the window quickly, pretending to be interested in the brick wall my window faced.

"What's going on, Lauli-gator?"

"Well, Hannah told me something bad today… she said Jimmy is telling people I'm here for slitting my wrists."

"Oh, Lau. What have I always told ya?"

And then she started shaking her booty and pointing her fingers at me singing, "Just give 'em somethin' to talk about!" misquoting the Bonnie Raitt song, like she normally did when my pre-teen world was filled with drama. I rolled my eyes at her swaying hips.

"I know…" I sighed.

"Seriously though, Lau, who cares what they say? Your friends know the real reason you're here, and life's too short to worry about what anyone else thinks. In a week, it will be old news, and you'll be back in school strutting your stuff."

She was right, and I let it roll off my shoulders, like I did with most things.

Life is too short to let the negativity bring you down, to let the words of others seep deep within you. You can choose to feel the hurt, to let it fester, to feel anger, and to drag out those feelings until you've expended all your energy on them. Or you can choose to recognize when you have little control over the assumptions people make. When people don't have all of the information, they fill the gaps in their mind with untrue stories, lies, and gossip. It isn't fair. It isn't nice, but you win when you refuse to let the words, and the made up stories, and the fear of what they are saying behind your back penetrate. And that's easy to do when you have a mom shaking her butt and giving you a hug.

Most of the time, the things people say are a reflection of their own insecurities, and have nothing to do with you. If you can't find it in yourself to be compassionate before you start casting blame on every person who does something cruel, you will drown in the negativity.

* * *

So as I continue to look at myself in the mirror, my skin taut against my bones, my hair greased back hiding the limp curls, the red bandage hiding what I know is an IV but my classmates have no idea, I could worry about a million assumptions my classmates will make. That I'm anorexic, that the bandage is hiding the scars of my self-mutilation, or that I didn't listen to the teachers who said drugs were bad. Tonight, I'm going to the dance and that's all that matters.

"Just give 'em something to talk about," I sing quietly, so Mom won't know I took her lesson to heart.

Rather than taking photos in front of our fireplace's mantle, we take them in front of the wooden door of the hospital bathroom. I turn to the side, tilt my pale face, and smile weakly—but inside I'm gushing. Nurses line up to wish me good luck, and my nurse stops in to check my blood pressure, temperature, and oxygen saturation one last time.

Soon, we are flying down I-93 in my chariot, my dad's green mini van, racing to get to the dance with moments to spare. Dad whips the van through the circle in front of the Gordan W. Mitchell Middle School, and I roll open the sliding door in the back. My silver heels click on the pavement, and Mom trails behind me, zippering her coat. I pull open both of the doors into the lobby, like they are the doors to my castle, and tell my mom to hang back. The dance is just starting, so my friends are in the lobby waiting to check in with the chaperone. They squeal when they see me, and tell me they love my dress. I squeal back with compliments to their hair, while Mom motions for us to squeeze together, peering through the viewfinder of her disposable camera. I smile weakly, being careful not to split my dry, cracked lips.

"Beautiful girls! Have fun!"

She turns to the chaperone, waving her hand to the kids behind her to get in line.

"I'm here if she needs anything."

I step into the tile-floored cafeteria, transformed into a night-club, with strobe lights and a disco ball hanging from the ceiling fan. Leaning against the wall is my 7th grade crush. He waves, smiles, and walks coolly over to me and my friends, his hands shoved into his pockets. Before I can say anything, he hugs me. After a few seconds of feeling my ribs crushed against his silky tie, he kisses me on the cheek.

"I'm so happy you're here, Lauren."

The DJ plays a slow Avril Lavigne song and we dance a little closer than one foot apart. And although I can still smell the latex mask that was on my face only a few hours earlier, it doesn't matter—this has been a truly great adventure, and it was all worth it.

How to Turn a Wimp into a Superhero

On my first day of college, single, heartbroken, and utterly unable to deal with all of the scary things that lie ahead, I try to channel my inner 7th grade self in her red sparkly dress. Strong. Unbreakable. Determined.

Of course, on move-in day, it's pouring. It's not the kind of rain that makes puddles to splash in. It makes streams to jump over. Dad hoists my big vest machine out of the backseat of the car. I'm weary of the cars around us as it slams to the ground and he begins to fumble with a plastic bag. He slips the black bag over the top of the machine, protecting its innermost workings from the destructive wetness that surrounds us.

Walking a few steps ahead of my dad wheeling my 30-pound medical device through the parking lot, I'm grateful for the rain. Had it been sunny, who knows the looks I'd get. "What's a college student use that for anyway?" I'd smile and avoid the questions, walk beside my dad and act like the bin I'm carrying that's filled to the brim with pill bottles is perfectly normal. Instead, I wrap another bag over the top of the bin... blending in with the rest of the students whose bins are filled with notebooks, pens, pencils, probably a handle of bottom shelf vodka hidden at the bottom that their big sister bought them for their first weekend at college. All the necessities.

I walk up to the front desk of the dormitory and say my name, "Lauren." A tall, skinny girl with bright red frizzy hair asks how to spell my last name, and plucks an envelope with it misspelled on the front.

"Okay, Lauren, you are in Boland, Room 127. I'm your RA, Rosie. Let me know if there is anything you need."

I mutter thanks and make my way down the hall, and breathe a sigh of relief when I see that my room is on the ground floor.

"Thank God we don't have to lug that thing up the stairs," I tell my Dad, wheeling my big machine behind me.

I open the door to see two beds, one already piled high with suitcases and boxes. Brielle turns when I enter and smiles.

"Here we are!"

I'm so happy we've already met and I've explained that I'd have a few more extra things than a typical roommate. When I told her I have cystic fibrosis she smiled and asked, "What's that?"

To which I gave her the dumb-downed version.

"It makes me cough a lot. So I have to take medicine and do therapy to ease my symptoms."

Later, the day after she gets a flu shot to protect my weak immune system from germs, she'd drunkenly tell her boyfriend, "it's like a mix between asthma and AIDS." We'd laugh about it. Eh, close enough. She nonchalantly answered, "Gotcha!" And it's as painless as that.

Carefully pulling off the trash bag, I present my vest like a magician presenting his rabbit.

"Here it is! The shaky thing I was telling you about."

She nods in recognition and suggests the perfect spot under our wall-length built-in desk.

* * *

When I was 7 years old, we packed up my bags for the first time, folding my new satin pajama pants with the frogs on them into my rolling backpack, tucked my pillow with the Lion King pillowcase into the back seat of the car, and drove to Children's for what would be a two-week hospital stay, on my first day of elementary school.

While the neighborhood kids dressed in their newest shoes and dresses, and took pictures getting onto the school bus, I stepped into a 10 by 10 hospital room for the first time, taking in the animal wallpaper, the funny looking bed in the shape of a chair, and the checkered curtain dividing the room, where another bed sat, waiting for its next guest.

That night, the nurse knocked on the door, opened it up, and introduced herself. She explained that she was here to insert a PICC line into my arm, which would deliver medication to me for the next two weeks. My mom pulled her chair to the side of the bed and held my hand, her soft hands squeezing mine tight, while the nurse went to work applying numbing medication. It hurt. I cried, and I still remember the fear and confusion that came with wondering what I was in for.

But there they were, my parents, right there. They ushered in visitors almost every day, presenting me with balloons, and toys, and crafts. They summoned the child life specialist for movies to watch at night, and Mom slept on the pull-out couch by my side.

My teachers had given me a packet of homework to stay up to date on my reading, and Mom and Dad helped me each day to complete it, along with the tutor who visited.

Finally, the two weeks ended and I was wheeled down to the car, ready to face the world.

Mom dressed me in my best dress and new black shoes for my very own first day of school, two weeks late. She took pictures like any first day of school, cried like any first day of school, and waited for the school bus like any first day of school.

But I remembered the last time I entered a new place, and a nurse shoved a needle in my arm! I remembered the last time I met new people, and they were sick, their parents seemed so unsure, and they smelled like urine. So I latched onto my mom. I cried and screamed and wouldn't enter that bus. Okay, so no bus today, my mom thought.

She loaded me into the mini-van, my backpack on my lap, and we drove to school together. Whereas some 7-year-olds would have shooed their parents away walking through the halls, I had no qualms about latching onto my mom.

"Pick me up!" I begged.

"No, Lauren. I can't pick you up. I'll hold your hand but you have to walk through the hall with me."

My teacher came to introduce herself, and I shoved my head into the back of Mom's legs. Miss B had bright blue eyes that welcomed me into her colorful classroom, with fish pinned to a bulletin board displaying each of the 18 students' names.

"This one is yours," she said, pointing to a blue fish with a sparkly scale, from *The Rainbow Fish* book I had read in the hospital.

With one hand balled into a fist around Mom's pant leg, and the other tentatively holding Miss B's finger, she guided us over to the reading corner where a few students sat flipping through picture books.

"Your Mom has to go to work now," Miss B explained. "If you want to hold my hand today, you can go right ahead."

I sniffled, wiped my tears on my dress sleeve, and gave Mom a hug goodbye.

It took a few days of this for me to go willingly into Miss B's arms, who was waiting at the doorway for a hug. Once Mom felt confident I could walk down the halls without begging her to pick me up, she tried the bus.

That day, I squeezed her legs at the bus stop, half jittering with excitement to finally ride the big yellow school bus, half nervously biting my hair. When the bus pulled up, my best friend and next-door neighbor, Taylor, skipped up the school bus steps. I stepped forward and looked back at my mom, tears forming in the corner of my eyes. She gently pushed me up the steps and I begged her to drive me just one more time.

"Lauren, you have to go on the bus. You can sit with Taylor all the way there, and Miss B will be at the end of the hall like she is every day. It's going to be okay. Who loves ya baby?"

She looked up at the school bus driver as she shoved my little bum up the steps.

"I really am a good mother."

"I know you are," the bus driver said.

Telling this story today, Mom describes how gut wrenching it was to push me onto the first step of the school bus. She could have driven me to school that day, and every single day after that, but if she didn't allow me to face the uncertainty, to build up my own bravery, and to cope with that on my own

– how would I have ever become courageous? She knew my teacher would make me feel at ease, that there were nice little kids willing to play on the playground, and that I was strong. It took a few more days here and there of tears, latching on, and my own unwillingness to face the fear. But gently, she reminded me of what a big girl I was. Yes, I had this scary illness and had just come from a scary place, but she believed I had the bravery within me to walk down the hall on my own.

* * *

Today though, there is no way in hell I am latching onto my Mom, not if I want to have any friends on my first day of school. So I tell them they can go, and she bursts into tears. I give her a hug, and this time I tell *her* to stop her crying.

"I'll be fine, Mom! Who loves ya, Mama Bear?"

She walks down the hall with Dad, and I get to work on unpacking my boxes. I hear a knock on the door, and open it up to find my new friend, Kyle.

I met him at Freshman Orientation only a few months before, when high school seniors came to Stonehill to get acquainted with campus, and play corny ice breaker games the whole time to get to know one another. I was sitting in a room with our orientation group, The Sweet and Sour Royal Ducks, and looked around at each member of the group. Kyle sat directly across from me, his reddish blond hair flowing out around his ears, wearing a blue shirt.

Our leaders had us go around the room and say our name, with an adjective that describes us using the first letter of our name. I say "Lovely Lauren," and Kyle says "Kind Kyle," which is who he becomes the rest of our day at orientation.

The first game we played involved getting the group to line up in order of our birthdays without saying a word. We motioned to each other, holding up the number of fingers that corresponded to our birthdays. I held up a hand of five and a hand of three to Kyle, and he held up his own hand of five and three. Then, I put down my hand of three and pointed to the hand of five. He did the same. Next, he tried to tell me the year by holding up a random combination of fingers and, confused, I just stood next to him, laughing at the fact that we have the same birthday.

We started our second corny game, called Wagon Wheel, where we formed two concentric circles facing one another. We faced a new person every time the leader told us to switch, and then discussed a newly assigned topic. The first time I faced Kind Kyle, we were supposed to be talking about where we are from.

"I'm from Maine," Kyle said.

"Oh, so you must ski!"

"Well, I snowboard. But yeah!"

We spent the next five minutes bonding over our love of snow, how we had both skied Sunday River mountain, and how this past ski season was amazing with all the snow we got. The leader told us time was up and we switched to the next person.

Soon, we'd gone around the entire circle, and stood in front of one another again. The leader read off the topic and we ignored it.

"What's your favorite trail at Sunday River?" I asked.

And so we continued our previous conversation.

Now, I'm unpacking my boxes and Kind Kyle is standing in my room, leaning against the bureau next to the door.

"How was your summer?" I ask, trying to distract from the fact that I'm unpacking my underwear.

It was a little awkward, but I'm happy I have a friend on my first day of college. And he's kind of cute.

So What?!

Every year, as a family, we head up and stay at my aunt and uncle's condo in New Hampshire. I love going there. They have eight kids, and my cousin Theresa and I are the youngest of all of them. Entertainment fills the walls of the condo, boys rough-housing, girls playing games, and the older kids stomping the snow from their ski boots after a long day of skiing with the adults.

My favorite thing to do is to go to the Recreation Center (or the Rec Cent-ah as we call it) and swim all day. After we get home, my mom sings, as she usually does, "it's treatment time!" It's time to plug into my nebulizer and for my dad to perform chest PT. As a kid, it feels so weird to do my normally private treatments in front of my cousins, so I put it off.

She finds an outlet for my nebulizer next to the table, squirts medicine into the cup, and hands it to me.

"But we're about to play Go Fish," I whine.

Today, I flat out tell Mom I don't want to do it in front of my cousins.

"So what if you do it in front of them?!" she says. "Look, we will all play games together while you do your treatments."

It's something my mom says in order to remind me that you have to let things roll off your shoulder. "So What?!" What she's really doing is holding my hand while I come to terms with my fears. Knowing they might stare, which would make me uncomfortable, she makes it fun. So not only am I at ease with something I'm afraid and uncertain about, but my cousins see that it isn't a big deal.

Reluctantly I comply, and Mom lists off games I can easily play while tilted upside down on the couch pillows. We play 20 Questions, guessing the animals we were thinking of, iSpy—and inevitably get laughing about the tootsie roll Shelly put under her little brother in the hot tub, screaming, "Dave pooped in the hot tub!"

If she had let me give in to my fears, and allowed me to do my chest PT behind closed doors, I would have continued to hide behind my fear of being different, of facing my cf head on, and of dealing with the awkward moments that came with all of that. If she didn't say, "So What," the limitations my fear created would have remained just that—limitations. Saying, "So What," was preparing me for each moment when I would face those fears, rather than hide behind them. It knocked down the wall that felt so safe to put up when it came to explaining my condition to people. As a kid, saying I had cf was like telling you my favorite color was purple. The depth and the nuances that came with having a life-threatening illness were not yet apparent to me in those days, so it became old hat.

But as I got older and began to note the responses I received, and most importantly, recognized what pity looked and sounded like, I got more sheepish about this matter-of-fact manner of telling people. Soon, it became almost a defensive conversation, where I was hell bent on making the person not feel so bad about what I just told them.

It would go something like this:

New coworker: "Geesh, Lauren, that cough isn't going away, huh? Poor thing."

Me: "Well, actually, I have cystic fibrosis, a lung disease which makes me cough a lot... have you heard of it?"

New coworker: "I had no idea! I'm so sorry. I... uh... knew someone with it."

(Past tense... here it comes.)

Me: "Yeah, it can be a pretty scary disease. But it affects people differently. I've lived with it my whole life and there are xyz drugs being studied now."

BIG SMILE, BIG SMILE to disarm the sad eyes I'm getting.

New coworker: "I didn't realize... you look so great."

Me: "Yeah, I've been lucky."

It was during the small moments of living the "So What" life that would allow me to realize how silly it was to get upset, to harp on the smallest problems, and to instead move on and get through it. Of course, living the "So What" life didn't mean ignoring my emotions, or that I was expected to just get over the big issues, but it allowed me to see some issues as inevitable. In times when you don't have a choice, it helps to think about what you need to do to get through, and what you've got within you to do it. When I was nervous about doing my vest in front of my cousins, and just wanted to play games, living the "So What" life let me have fun with them, and show them that it was no big deal… just a small piece of my life.

And even though my mom never explicitly said "So What" when I had to, say, go into the hospital, I soon learned to get on with my life while I was there, too. I'd joke, "Woo-hoo, I don't have to go to school!" or, "It's just an excuse to get presents!" Even though it was hard, humor was a positive coping mechanism for me, and to this day, when I'm not able to control my situation, the least I can do is say "So What" and think of everything I have in my power to live despite what is going on.

That means when I needed to be on strong antibiotics—that made me sensitive to the sun—while on vacation with my friends in the Caribbean, I bought a "sexy" swimming shirt, rocked my hat in the pool, and slathered myself up with sunscreen. Someone else might have cancelled their trip, or spent all of their time indoors rather than being caught dead in a long-sleeved shirt in the pool, but I had no other option. I could miss out on the fun parts of my vacation, or say, "I'm on sunburn causing antibiotics in one of the places in the world where the sun is the strongest… 'So What!'" And from there, I make a plan of how I'll deal with it.

But really, what is the "So What" life? It's acknowledging the fear that holds you back from doing the things that are truly good for you. It's confronting the excuses you make that hold you back from living your best life. It's a challenge to rationality, a provocation to realism, and a punch in the face to the control your disease, or your mean boss, or your daily annoyance tries to take.

But saying "So What" is also about not taking things so seriously. You don't have time to take things so seriously. You're in the hospital, "So What?" That doesn't mean you can't laugh, make jokes at your own demise, check out the hot doctors, or feel the tiniest bit thankful that you get to watch talk shows all morning.

I once had a doctor who was in training. He went through the list of questions I was asked every single morning by at least three different doctors.

"Any pain? Any fevers? Does this hurt? How 'bout this? How are you pooping?"

I rattled off my responses.

"You know," he said, "the next time someone asks you that, you should ask: How are YOU pooping?"

"So What?" Be lighthearted. Ask doctors how they are pooping. The "So What" life is about redefining what's allowed in the midst of a shitty situation... pun intended. "So What?" Laugh. "So What?" Dance. "So What?" Question your excuses, question what society tells you your limitations should mean, and surprise yourself. Saying "So What" is tough. It sounds harsh. But sometimes you need tough love to get fear to loosen its grips.

Why TMI is Always a Good Thing

"This is my vest," I explain through the mouthpiece of the nebulizer in my mouth, a life-jacket-like vest wrapped around my small, slightly hunched torso, shaking faster and faster when my little hand turns the dial.

"It shakes my lungs cause I have stistic-fy-ro-sis."

The kids in my fifth grade class, Sarah, Hillary, John, are laughing, their eyes glued to me with fascination. I feel like Dr. Spark up here with my high-tech equipment, explaining something my peers know nothing about.

Last week, our class went on a field trip to the science museum. When we entered the "Electricity" exhibit at the Museum of Science, the lights were turned down and we heard a man talking on the floor beneath the balcony. We heard the whirring of the wheel he was cranking to build up static electricity on a large metal ball. He was standing there, with a name-tag that read "Dr. Spark," a lab coat, wild gray hair, one hand grasping the large metal ball, the other in a fist pointed at the audience.

"I need a fearless volunteer!"

John raised his hand.

"Come on up!" said Dr. Spark, with an exaggerated gesture.

He instructed John to raise his hand in a fist like his. In a second, a huge spark flashed between Dr. Spark's and John's fists. All the kids in our class gasped, some screamed, some looked a little scared. But after a while, everyone was lined up. One by one, our class got a thrill out of the little shock between their tiny fist and the fist of the scientist. They went back to their friends, comparing stories: "Mine hurt!" "Yeah right! It felt GOOD!" "You're a baby!" "That was AWESOMEEEE!"

My classmates' faces are a little like that today. Some are afraid, some fascinated, some giggle nervously. At the end of my explanation, Mrs. McDonald smiles, tears welling up in her eyes.

"That was excellent, Lauren. Now, who has questions?"

A few hands shoot up.

"Is it fun?"

"Does it hurt?"

I shrug and laugh and answer their questions, feeling empowered by my knowledge of cf, the topic I chose for my first research paper.

This was something my parents instilled in me. My mom, the nurse, and my dad, the nurse by association and extensive researching skills, never hesitate to tell people about cf, and even invite questions: what it was, why I did my treatments, what my latest test result meant, updating them about new advances. When in doubt, Mom always gave TMI (too much information). The fact that they are the opposite of private actually helped me to become more comfortable with my illness, and helped to educate my friends and family about what everything meant. That's why I didn't flinch when I realized that doing a report on my own illness would mean bringing a very private piece of my life into the classroom. In fact, I was excited about it: a chance to tell all my friends about something they didn't know about, something I happened to know a lot about.

Creating a space where people are comfortable learning more is so important when dealing with an illness, particularly when it isn't apparent from the outside what is going on. Disclosing my illness *and* educating people about how it affects me is important to me; I've seen first hand the assumptions and hurt that comes with not telling someone.

In high school, I made it a point to tell every teacher about my cystic fibrosis at the beginning of the year. So that when the inevitable came about, whether it be a hospitalization, a doctor's appointment, a question about my health, there were to be no assumptions. One year, though, I made the mistake of withholding the information from a teacher who oversaw my study period.

His name was Bob Perkins. He was a rough and tumble guy with a thick Boston accent who had wrinkles around his eyes from joking with his students *and* yelling at the hockey players he coached.

That winter was especially rough for me. I caught a cold that never went away, and it had settled deep into my lungs. My cough was almost constant, the infection irritating it into a dry, tight, wheezy tunnel. In the silent study hall it's all you heard. One day, Mr. Perkins had enough. It started out friendly and well-meaning.

"I have cough drops, Lauren."

Since cough drops aren't always the best option, I politely declined. Cough suppressants aren't good for people with cf because you're coughing for a reason, to get the mucus out. When you suppress the cough, the mucus stays, and that is the opposite of what you want to do.

A few days passed. I walked into study hall and opened up my English book to read a short story. He walked over and plopped a full bag of cough drops on my desk.

"I can't stand it any more! Here."

My stomach dropped, a lump diving from my throat into my intestine, splashing up tears into my eyes. I blinked them back, grabbed the cough drops, and marched to the door. I slammed it behind me and rushed to the bathroom, tears building with each step. I approached the door and slowed down to compose myself, in case someone I knew was behind the door. To my relief, the bathroom was empty, so I slam dunked the cough drop bag into the trash and locked the stall door behind me. The tears came fast and hard, uncontrollable sobs shook my body, and I cursed fucking Bob Perkins under my breath. He was now my enemy, on my shit list, and I promised I'd go through the rest of the year avoiding any communication with him. I heard the bell ring so I quickly inhaled and wiped away the tears, tossed water on my face to wash away the red hint that I was upset. I smiled in the mirror to practice for the hallway, and the door swung open to a swarm of freshmen gossiping.

Checking to make sure he was down the hall in his normal spot talking to the history teacher, I snuck into the classroom to gather my things for third period and we never spoke about it again.

At the time, Bob Perkins was pure evil, and nothing could convince me otherwise. But, this wasn't one of the moments that you let roll off your shoulder. Had I been brave after that first offer of a cough drop, I could have used it as an opportunity to let him into my world. I failed to take responsibility to advocate for myself and educate him. I stayed silent, and keeping it a secret blew up in my face, and caused me to cast blame on someone who knew nothing about my situation, and who I couldn't have expected to know.

You alone have the power to shape what other people say and think about you, so when you let them make assumptions, they will say things that hurt your feelings. Giving TMI might feel like an invasion of privacy, but you get to take the reigns back in those situations so the person understands exactly what your child's life is like. And as the parent, you are setting the example for your child and sending them the message that it's okay to advocate and educate. This a valuable tool and will set up your child for success when people like Bob Perkins walk into their life.

Be Brave

Disclosing my illness became harder the more time I spent in the hospital, the hoarser and breathier my voice got, the more tired I was at the end of the day—real reminders that this disease wasn't a sissy, the symptoms weren't going away, and it was only going to get worse. In 5th grade, it was easy to show my classmates the very tangible vest and explain the pills I took, the doctors I visited, and the fact that the hospital had its own Pac-Man arcade game you didn't have to put coins into. What I didn't explain, because I hadn't yet experienced it, was the fact that my disease was freaking scary, took people's lives, and put very real barriers on mine. So as a teenager, when I had to talk about cf in a way that wasn't so straight-forward, I lost it.

In high school, all of the smart kids avoided electives. Our honors and AP credits weighted our GPA's more, so if you took an elective, which was at the level of "college prep," you risked lowering your GPA. An A in shop was lower than an A in AP Calculus. But I needed to write, so I put the GPA aside and took creative writing.

In general, I am shameless. I talk about my unshaven legs with friends, admit when it was me who farted, and once, when I landed flat on my ass trying to flip a hacky sack over my head in between classes, I laughed harder than my friends did.

But the subject of my creative writing poem is one thing that sends blood to my face, makes my hands shake and my heart feel like it's being projected out of a megaphone—just like when I couldn't bear the thought of doing my treatments in front of my cousins. I'm sitting in the "on deck" chair while my classmate reads his poem, a description of what sounds like a Playboy Bunny, but turns out to be his pickup truck. When he reveals the subject of his poem the class laughs, but I'm too busy wiping my sweaty palms on my jeans. I can feel the heat in my red face, and I'm surprised, because someone could pants me in front of everyone and I would do a little dance in my underpants before pulling them back up to the applause.

Just a week before, as we were polishing up our poems and putting on the finishing touches, I met in the hallway with my creative writing teacher. He had already read through my poem.

"You're really brave you know," he said.

And he didn't have to say anything else. I knew that writing about my own illness required an immense amount of courage, and reading it in front of class would require even more.

It's go time. I stand, take a deep breath, and read my poem. I need to clear my throat, but know the cough will only release the fear, that my head might fly off and all the emotions, embarrassment, and discomfort will flow into the room in a million words that everyone will somehow know how to put together. Instead, I breathe.

"If I never had cf, I'd be a little taller."

I read each word, willing my voice to stop shaking.

"My…" my tongue meets the tip of my mouth between my two front teeth to pronounce, "lungs," and I choke a little, clearing my throat.

"…a little fuller. My skin a tad less salty. If I never had cf, I'd have stories for grandkids, beautiful wrinkles around my eyes."

I continue reading about all the things I would be without cf: selfish, ungrateful, but maybe fearless. At the end, I grit my teeth to pronounce, "Disease," and let the silence soak in. From my stool, I see people biting their lips, some drumming their pencils, others shuffling their papers, worrying more about their poems than mine. I look at their hands, not their eyes, because I know their eyes will be too sad, the pity spilling out like an overfilled glass of beer.

I close my eyes, lowering the flood-gates, and open them to see my teacher smiling at his grade book, which we all know is bull shit. I walk back to my seat and no one says a word, except to snap, like our teacher told us people do at poetry readings.

It is one of the bravest days of my life.

A week later, my teacher tells me that the editors of *The Viking Saga*, the semi-annual creative writing publication, chose my poem to be published. On the day it's released, kids grab copies of it from the table in the cafeteria and flip through it while eating their Dominos pizza. While walking back from lunch, up the four stories of stairs, a few people catch up to me and say, "Hey, that was a really great poem, ya know."

If you alone want to tell your story, you have to be brave.

Responsibility

The first night at college, in our hallway meeting with Rosie, I need to announce to the girls that I have cf, since sometimes they might see me doing my vest in my room, or cleaning my nebulizers in the bathroom. At the end of the meeting, Rosie asks if there is anything anyone would like to share. I raise my hand.

"I just want to let you all know that I have cystic fibrosis. It's no big deal, but sometimes you might see me with a weird machine in my room!"

I shrug it off and smile like I've learned to do so many times when people start avoiding eye contact, as if their pity would stab me in the heart if they looked. As people do, they politely nod, and another girl tells the group about her latex allergy. Later, Brielle asks me if that means we can't use condoms.

"Maybe just not put balloons on our doors for our birthdays," I offer.

Before college, I had planned to live in a single room.

"Or maybe you could find a nice deaf girl to room with you," Mom mused one morning while I did my vest and nebulizers, raising her voice over the compressor's *whir*.

Having my own room would give me privacy, and allow me to do my treatments early in the morning without disrupting anyone. I would be able to sleep when I wanted, have cough attacks at night, steer clear of sick people, and even have my own bathroom for the unfortunate side effects of forgetting to take my enzyme pills with a meal. Most of all, I wouldn't have to explain the scarier details of my disease. I wouldn't have to be brave.

But after I met Brielle online (she posted a photo of herself at Friendly's on Stonehill Class of '09's Facebook page), I prioritized making friends over my privacy. After all, I had grown unafraid of being open about my illness. Soon enough, Brielle asked if I wanted to room together. I warned her about my loud vest, and all of the disruptions that come along with cf.

"I'm sure it will be fine!" she said.

The next morning, Brielle and I wake up at the same time and walk to the dining hall. After we tried out the cafeteria food, we walk back in the rain and I plug in my vest and nebulizer, open our mini refrigerator to retrieve my medication, and turn on the machine to show Brielle, while she looks at a map to find where her first class would be. My vest whirs to life, the air in the hoses beating like helicopter blades.

"Do you think you can sleep through this?" I ask.

"I'm sure I'll get used to it," she shrugs.

What I didn't know then, was that day was the start of adulthood. Where my health fell wholly upon my choices, my schedule, and my back.

In the weeks and months that follow, I enjoy college like any other kid in my dorm. We get drunk, me for the first time, and hide the empty handles in the ceiling tiles. We stay up late, become friends with strangers, and gossip. Determined to replace Mike, I throw myself at guys hoping one of them will stick. Each morning though, I do my vest. I'm enjoying this life too much to let myself get sick. I have a responsibility to continue to take care of myself, so I make sure to never skip a treatment. After all, that's all taking care of myself meant up until this point.

Let Them Be Stupid

When we first went to look at Stonehill, Mom and I sat and listened to the admissions counselors talk about the process of applying.

"And parents, I have to say this… when your child is applying and they have a question, I better not be hearing from you. Your kids are adults now!"

I giggled, my mom nudged me with her elbow, and smiled knowingly, as if to say, "Lauren, you are *definitely* gonna be the one making the calls."

Mom always trusted that I would get the job done. When parent/teacher conferences rolled around, she never called to schedule an appointment. Not because I was a problem child and she wanted to avoid hearing the bad news, but because she knew that I, the model student, was getting straight A's and would continue to work towards going to college.

One blessing of living with a very adult disease at a young age is that I learned quickly to do many things myself. I could open child proof pill bottles as a child myself, and knew every setting on my vest machine by heart. My parents taught my brothers and I, "how to fish." This meant we did our own laundry by high school. And they never cleaned our rooms for us, even if we let the toys and laundry pile up for weeks. We were expected to do our homework and try to solve the problem before we went asking Dad for help. They were small things, but they taught us to be independent.

From the moment we are young, we want to do it all by ourselves, and our parents can't bear the thought of how we'll ever face the world without them holding our hand, guiding us, and reminding us to turn in our homework.

My nephew is 2, and up until this point I've been convinced he hates me. It seems no matter what I do, I'm met with a resounding, "No!" As his older brother marches through the world of independence, little Will marches right behind him. We are at the beach, the sand perfectly soft without a rock in sight, the tide high enough to hide the smooth weathered ones beneath the surf, well beyond the sand bar that creates a haven for the two toddlers to play and splash. Seeing him wobble through the waves, I put out my hand for him to hold.

"No!" he wails, and pulls it away, jogging into the shallows and kicking his feet.

He laughs when I splash him with water, dancing through the waves. It is always so glorious to run away from the playful monster. It is freeing to escape on your own. Running deeper, chasing his brother, he trips like the wave he stepped on was a football, his balance wobbling until *KERPLAT*. He splashes into the sandy water, hands and face first. He looks up to gauge my reaction as I swoop him onto his feet.

"Oh no, buddy!"

"Nooo!" he wails, louder this time. "Dada?"

He whips his head in search of Dada's yellow t-shirt, pointing to the only one who can make it better. I carry him over, cold salt water soaking through my shirt.

Dada grabs him for a quick kiss. Immediately, the tears are turned off like the kitchen sink when the dishes are finally clean. Dada reminds him how much fun it was to chase his brother into the waves and he gets back to it, as if he had never fallen face first into their depths.

From the time we can walk, we are so determined to do so without guidance, pushing away the hands that try to hold our balance, determined to get there on our own. But when we fall, it's our parents we look to to tell us what is scary, what deserves a cry, what we should waste our stress on, and when it's okay to keep splashing.

Later on, I remark to my brother how funny it is that I am always met with a, "no," when confronting my little nephew.

"He likes to do things on his own these days."

Of course my little guy doesn't hate me; I was trying to take away his independence. He just wanted to run through the waves by himself, testing how deep he could go. He wanted to stand back up by himself, and even wanted to find his Dada when he needed him on his own. We sick kids want to go through life as independently as possible, free to wobble and *KERPLAT* on our own. The first few months of my freshman year in college, I was wobbling and *KERPLATing* all over the place. And I was no longer relying on Mom or Dad to tell me where the line was.

Kids learn from everything. Touch the hot oven, and you won't touch it again. Hit your brother in the face with a block and go without dessert, and you'll think twice next time. Each step we take as a wobbly baby we are learning. Step this way, hold your hands this way, and you'll move forward. Falling down is scary at first, but we babies figure out what we did wrong to end up on the ground. The decision you as a parent have to make is whether or not to hold out your hands to prevent us from falling, or to encourage us and give us kisses and hugs until we wobble our way into your arms, happy to run around in the world, even if it means taking a few spills along the way.

When your kid has a chronic illness, your instinct is to do everything you possibly can to keep them healthy. And to be fair, that instinct is born of love. You love your child, so why would you let them make a mistake that may cause them pain?

A parent once reached out to me because she was having a hard time believing that her grumpy teenager would ever grow up to be as positive and responsible as I made myself out to be in my blog. When I talked to her, I had to give her the hard truth: that responsibility didn't come easily. Though my parents had been priming me throughout my life to make decisions that would positively impact my life, it was ultimately up to me to figure it out on my own. That meant I would skip out on treatments sometimes, forget to take my pills, or worse, purposefully not take my pills, and be lax about the little things that could affect my health, like sleep, eating right, and exercising.

Of course, sometimes I get sick regardless of what I do. I'll catch a cold while standing in line at the mall behind a sniffling 2-year-old, and down the spiral I go. Or I'll acquire the deadly bacteria that makes it more difficult to fight the infection in my lungs. Sometimes when I got sick, it wasn't my fault. But a majority of the time… it was.

This is a controversial thing to say in the world of genetic, life-threatening illnesses, and it isn't true for everyone. After all, there are certain effects your malfunctioning cells have on your body that are beyond your control. But for each hospitalization, I could trace back to the better choices I could have made. I could have called the doctor sooner, taken a break when I felt my body getting run down, not skipped so many treatments that week, sterilized my nebulizers, exercised more, slept more, made better choices about what I ate. I could have stayed away from my sick friend or boyfriend. Personal responsibility, for me, is what turned me from a rebellious (used in the slightest sense of the word) teenager, into a mindful, take-charge-of-my-health adult.

All my life, my parents were setting me up to understand the delicate balancing act that is cystic fibrosis. I knew my lungs were filled with mucus and bacteria, and there were certain things I needed to do to keep that mucus and bacteria at bay. I knew when I didn't do those things I coughed more, felt more pain in my chest, and wanted to sleep more. But I also knew that when I didn't do those things I had more time to play with my friends, laugh with my brothers, and enjoy life, if only for an hour, sans cf. And my parents knew that, too.

Sometimes, on family vacation, the days of beach going and bike riding were over planned with fun, and my treatments were quickly forgotten about. And for that day, my parents didn't nag me. They let my vest and nebulizers sit beside the couch as if it were part of the decor, sharing a mutual understanding that this was one of those days where life took precedence. Tomorrow, the mucus in my lungs would stick like gum to the bottom of your shoe, so maybe we would lay low. And definitely, my vest and nebulizer would whir to life in the morning, shaking away yesterday's decision.

Where kids (okay, teenagers) make mistakes, is not knowing exactly when life takes precedence. They think their lives, that seem overrun with their illness, are for being a teenager, not for spending time doing silly things like keeping themselves alive so they can safely gossip with friends, make risky choices, and hate their parents. No, to a teenager, the line between letting yourself be imperfect for the sake of a quality of life, and doing all you can to keep yourself healthy for the sake of a quality of life gets blurred. It gets more than blurred—someone dices it up into a 1000-piece puzzle, flips over the pieces to the cardboard side, and says, "Okay, figure it out."

For me, unfortunately, it was a near-death experience at the age of 15 that *began* to solidify the line. I'd like to say that coughing up pints of blood, watching ten doctors rush into my room as machines beeped telling them I was going into shock, and spending the night in the ICU, where I was given the anointment of the sick, was enough to tell me where the line was.

You would think an experience like that would serve to tell me I had grossly miscalculated where it was, and had chartered myself too far off course to even show up on the radar. But, teenagers, my dears, are idiots.

That winter, several weeks before the Great Blood Geyser of 2005, I had spent a couple weeks in the hospital, which looking back I can attribute to a solid month or two of skipping out on treatments. While my lungs were filling with infection, the ground beneath Children's Hospital was filling with two feet of snow. Nurses were staying the night in empty hospital beds. All I wanted to do was drive around our neighborhood and witness the piles of snow above my waist, feel the energy from the kids next door racing their sleds up and down the dead end road, and maybe make a snow angel.

By the time I got out of the hospital, the snow had turned brown and melty, nothing like it had been when the newswoman stood in the deep, white, powdery snow, struggling to pull her leg out from under it. After signing papers to go home, my IV still in my arm, prepared for another week of antibiotics, we drove through the mucky streets of Boston, then the highway soaked in salt and sand. When we turned into the quaint neighborhoods of our small town I saw snowmen drooping, rivers running down the street into the sewer drains, and the blackened snow at the end of our driveway.

When I was in the hospital, I dreamed of wading through the waist-deep snow, building igloos, and sledding with my friends. Instead, my lungs decided they would create their own natural disaster, flooding with blood, and instilling in me a fear that I might never get the chance to wade through deep piles of snow again.

For the first time in my life, I made a connection in one of the synapses in my thick skull. If I didn't get it together, cf could kill me. It was the first time I realized I was not invincible nor immune. This was one of the harsh realities my mom had taken pains to be so honest with me about. Though, she never quite used those words. She made gentle connections. IF you don't do your treatments, THEN you'll be back in the hospital. IF you don't get your rest today, THEN you'll feel like crap tomorrow. And sometimes what she meant was maybe you'll feel like crap forever.

It's a funny little dance we do. You can't say outright that we are personally responsible when we get sick. You can't attribute too much responsibility to us chronically ill kids; there's only so much we can do before our illness wipes us out, despite our efforts. And if you put too much blame on us for our choices and mistakes, then our own sickness, then even our own death becomes our fault... and of all the things we could think, you don't want that.

The fact is, there is *some* responsibility to not dick around with death. There is responsibility to not be reckless, to do the stuff that science, and our doctors, and our bodies tell us will let us live a bit longer, feel a bit better, and be more of ourselves for the people who love us in the short time we have on this earth.

Where that responsibility blurs, though, is when it butts heads with life. Everyone has their own spectrum where health trumps living, and where living trumps health; between where the current moment takes precedence and where tomorrow takes precedence. By the time I reached college, I had a good grasp of where my health fell on my spectrum, slowly sliding closer to Priority #1.

But as I said, teenagers are idiots. So it took one more hard lesson to get me to the point where I understood the true meaning of personal responsibility.

When Life Karate Chops
You in the Knees

Freshman year, I do what any college student does. Not only do I gain the Freshman 15, I also learn the intricacies of how to sneak alcohol into my dorm room without alerting the Resident Assistants. I learn to wrap empty bottles in paper towels and plastic bags, as to not draw attention to the trash cans. I stay up way past when I am tired, study just enough to feel stressed that I might not pass my test, but get an A anyways, and grapple with the fact that I, and only I, am in control of my health. One thing remains constant though: I always find time to do my vest. Still, I don't exercise much, and keep pushing on to keep up with the social pace of college life, way beyond the point my body can handle.

One day, hooked up to my vest, sitting at my desk half doing homework, half chatting with friends on AOL Instant Messenger, I get a chat from my old buddy, Faith.

"Hey kiddo! How's college treating ya?"

"I love it! My friends are so great, they even hang out with me while I do my vest LOL! Stonehill is so pretty in the fall, too. How are ya doing?"

"In the hole again, got a nasty bug this time around."

The timer on my vest *dings* and I check the clock: it's 12:00. Time for lunch already, and it's Pastabilities (my favorite cafeteria meal, where you put anything you please in your pasta… including bacon), so I have to run to get in line.

"Aww bummer. Feel better, Faith. Is the cute docta at least on this time?"

She LOL's. I can hear her raspy laugh in my head.

"Hey I gotta go grab lunch, ttyl! <3"

Faith was the first person I talked to online with cf. Because cf lungs culture so much scary bacteria, people with cf aren't supposed to hang around each other for fear of inviting unexpected guests into our lungs… the kind that don't leave. My cousin worked with her and asked if she could give her my screenname so we could chat. I was excited to virtually meet someone who knew all about the world of hospitals, enzymes, and chest PT. A couple days later, my instant messenger account was pinging with a message from her.

The internet and instant messaging opened up a whole new world for me, where I wasn't the only one who coughed up boatloads of mucus. To top it off, Faith was *old*—as people with cf go—she was in her 50s! Her age gave me hope that I had a whole lot of living left to do. We chatted about how much we hate hospital food, and shared our favorite nurses and doctors. When I was admitted to the hospital at the same time as her during high school, I stood in her doorway and she sat on her bed, bouncing up and down and waving, shouting in her raspy voice, "HI, LAUREN!"

During that stay, the skeleton of a new 10-story building towered outside our windows, the rusty steel beams marking each floor. Kids up and down the Children's inpatient units wrote their names on signs and taped them to their windows. The construction workers repelled down the steel structure to spray paint their names in bright orange graffiti, their names living on in the new hospital wing that would save more lives, and hold the hands of those it couldn't.

That morning, I sat by the window and watched the construction worker repel down to the empty steel beams. He shook the can and painted an "F," then an "A," spelling out FAITH in all capital letters, bright orange. On the way to physical therapy, I stopped outside the open door of her room.

"Faith! You're famous!"

She pointed to the sign on her window.

"My nurse made me do it!" she said mischievously, clenching her teeth and laughing devilishly.

Though we only met through open doors and long hallways, Faith was a connection to my future. She was living, breathing proof of a long life with cf, and she lived it with zest and humor.

One night, freshman year of college, Mom picks me up from school to have dinner at home and the phone rings, my cousin's name flashing on the Caller ID. I hear my mom on the phone.

"Oh Sheila, that's awful. I had no idea… yeah. Well, thanks for calling."

I know that tone, the way my mom pauses and shakes her head. And when she tells me it's Faith, it might as well have been me. The bacteria lurking in my lungs, the same bacteria that had settled into Faith's lungs, was unforgiving. And if Faith wasn't safe from it, neither was I. Life shits on everything that night by killing my first friend with cf.

A few days later, life continues to karate chop me in the knees.

I feel the familiar wave of fatigue and fever and know it's time to call the doctor when I can't finish my Pastabilities. Mom meets me at school to make the drive into Children's to do Pulmonary Function Tests to measure my lungs. My doctor listens to my lungs and runs through a list of symptoms. Fatigue? Check. Loss of appetite? Check. Feeling out of breath? Check.

"Lauren, I definitely think you would benefit from a clean-out."

Otherwise known as a couple weeks of potent IV antibiotics delivered eight times a day.

"I would love to get you in this week."

On the way home, I know it's inevitable, but I still wish I could just go back to school and hang out with my friends and be a normal college freshman. Of all the things I should have been worrying about, I'm thinking about how this would be a setback in my quest to find a boyfriend. Faith's death had given me a sense of immediacy, like I was wasting time. I was still single, and I needed to get on with cramming in all I could in this short life. How would I make it through college if it only took three months to get sick?

The next day, I move out of my dorm for two weeks so I can get another PICC line to deliver intravenous medication. I have FOMO (fear of missing out) worse than ever before. To help cure it, my friends send me photos every day to keep me informed of everything I have been missing. They even stop by one night and stay for hours, filling me in on all the happenings at school: who is dating who, who stopped being friends, and about the boys on the second floor they've been hanging out with, including Kind Kyle.

Even though everyone tries their best to keep my spirits up with visits, good food, cards, chocolate, and fruit bouquets, I am down in the dumps. It isn't their responsibility to help me come to terms with my own illness; I have to look within to find what I need to get through this.

So here I am, on my parent's couch, missing out on college, clicking through photos my friends posted on my Facebook wall telling me how much they miss me, all because I have failed to treat my body the way I am supposed to. This was a clear-cut line of personal responsibility. Yes, cf is relentless. Yes, the bacteria in my lungs is deadly, but that doesn't mean I have permission to be irresponsible. Merely doing my vest and taking my medications isn't enough. I have to get more rest than I'm getting. I have to stop trying to keep up with my friends in drinking and staying up late. And I have to start exercising again. I have to improve my quality of life by doing the things I know will keep me healthy. My mom has told me that in less direct words my entire life. But I had to come to the realization on my own.

Choose to Be Honest

I'm in sixth grade at a regular appointment at Children's Hospital, to get my lungs tested and check in with my doctor. While listening to my lungs, feeling my stomach, and peeking in my ears and nose, my doctor mentions that there was an outbreak of a dangerous bacteria among cf patients called Burkholderia Cepacia, so they are testing everyone, "out of an abundance of caution." I cough up some mucus, spit it into a cup, and it's sent off to the lab.

On the car ride home I ask my mom questions about it. What is it? What would it mean? How did everyone get it?

She isn't sure. This is a bacteria she knows little about, except that it is the one bacteria you absolutely didn't want to get. People talk about it in hushed whispers in the cf community, and people who have it aren't allowed to attend certain events. They might pass it on to each other, our mucus-filled lungs like glue for the deadly bugs. Not one to worry until she has to, my mom tells me not to worry too much, and we head off to get dinner like we always do after these appointments.

"We don't know if you have it. So let's prepare for the worst. And hope for the best. That way, we won't be disappointed."

It's a mindset we use a lot. Mom says these words before doctor's appointments, when, let's be honest, we both know my coughing and lack of energy will mean we're going to be making a trip to the hotel Children's Hospital. And they're spoken when I wait anxiously for news of my release from the hospital. Prepare for the worst, hope for the best. But in most instances, what she really means is *expect* the worst.

I learned early on that being optimistic often led to being let down. For someone with such a positive attitude about my illness, this seems counterintuitive, but it was something I had to come to grips with sooner or later. As I learned what my symptoms meant, I knew how to prepare myself.

The best quality I have is my realism, the ability to set expectations for myself: to know I might feel worse before I feel better, that there will be people who say they'll visit who will inevitably get too busy, that I had better count on two weeks and plan for three, and that, inevitably, a doctor, nurse, or physical therapist will interrupt a really funny episode of Ellen DeGeneres. With realism, it's so important to acquaint it with your friend, positivity, unless you want to find yourself moping about the world expecting that nothing good will come of any of this.

Sometimes people tune me out when I start to talk about positivity in the midst of everything that's going on. Most people mistake positivity for optimism, though, which has a bad rep for being naive, unrealistic, and the (cute) mistake of children.

See, realism assumes that the outcome is going to be dismal, the prognosis bad. But with positivity on your side, your attitude won't suffer; you'll refuse to lay down on your back and let realism kick you while you're down. Positivity is about looking around when you're trapped in a room with no windows, and being pumped that a sliver of light snuck in through a crack in the ceiling. Optimism says, there will be a window there tomorrow, I just know it.

Positivity is dancing in the rain, optimism is hoping it won't rain. Optimism is avoidance. Positivity is acceptance. Optimism says, "everything is gonna be okay." Positivity says, "everything isn't okay, but that's okay." Because at least you have your family by your side, a fuzzy blanket, and Ellen DeGeneres to make you laugh.

However, optimism *is* hopeful. The mistake people make when being optimistic is they use it to wish for an unrealistic outcome, rather than using it to believe in their own power to impact the outcome. I can be optimistic that I'll have the mental and physical strength to make it through another bout of sickness, but only if my friend reality knows I really do have the strength within me, and only if my friend positivity lets me laugh about it and be thankful for a day to rest when I don't.

That night on the news, the pretty newscaster stands outside the familiar sign of Children's Hospital, reporting on the cepacia outbreak.

"Thirty-five cystic fibrosis patients here at Children's Hospital Boston were infected with a rare, antibiotic-resistant bacteria."

Images of patients wearing masks flash across the screen.

"Experts are still unsure what caused the outbreak, but are quick to point out that this bacteria is only dangerous to those with the disease, as it thrives in the mucus in their lungs."

A computerized image of what I imagine the inside of my lungs to look like appears, the camera zooming down a digestive tract like the Magic Schoolbus, filled with yellow globs of mucus seeming to reach out and grab the purple bacteria-looking-thing. Mom and Dad watch intently, guessing about how the bacteria might have spread: the PFT machine, the inpatient computer lab, the buttons on the elevators. I watch silently, remembering not to worry until I have to.

The day the doctor calls to say I cultured Burkholderia Cepacia, realism holds my hand tight and positivity sits on my shoulder, hiding behind my head, getting ready to peak out and say, "I'm going to teach you about appreciating life in the most complicated way I know how."

Though, as a 12-year-old, I don't have the wherewithal to understand the magnitude of what my doctor just told my mom, the partnership of realism and positivity is vital to the conversation my mom and I have next.

"Lauren," she takes a breath. "You have that bacteria."

"Well, what does that mean?"

"It's a pretty scary bacteria, like he said, but," (but is a word we use when we're about to be positive), "we'll just have to take it day by day."

And though she isn't unrealistically optimistic, she *is* real. She doesn't know what we are going to do about it, what it will mean for me, or that it is possible to be optimistic, or hopeful. She only knows we can't worry for the future when we are living in the moment, right now, faced with uncertainty and a deadly bacteria she knows is killing people with cf every single day—while also faced with the fact that I am very much alive and very much 12 years old.

So we take it day by day, realistically. And each day, we find something to be happy about, because what use would it be to worry today when we have our health, one another, and an episode of Ellen to dance to?

Robyn's Book

Back at home during my freshman year clean-out, I'm sitting at my desk next to my purple beaded curtains, PICC line hooked up to an IV pole, writing. Writing about how hard it is to lose a friend who has just died from the same bacteria that festers in my own lungs, how much I miss being at school, and how unsure I am about whether I'll even make it through college. Realism is shoving the breath out of me. How can I be positive when life is proving that I don't have what it takes, that I'm defenseless, and that I have to hold all this on my shoulders with no one to help share it?

In all my teenage melodrama, I think about the person I told these feelings to when they crept up in high school. Mike. Thinking back to what he told me a couple years before, I open up instant messenger, and type my ex-boyfriend's screenname into the send box.

"Can you Skype?"

* * *

We are sitting at the edge of my twin bed after school sophomore year of high school. Mike reaches for his backpack, unzips the zipper, rummages through his text books, and pulls out the book I had lent him. *Robyn's Book*, written by a teenager with cystic fibrosis, who reveals her truest feelings about the difficulty of life with a chronic, life-threatening illness. In the book, her friend with the disease passes away, and she copes with the realities of her short life while simultaneously displaying the wisdom gained from such experiences. In short, the book had managed to change my life in just three long nights.

Each night I would slip into bed with my pink pen, turning page after page and crying tear after tear, underlining my favorite parts, and double-underlining my most favorite. Those double-underlines reached deep into my heart, took out a piece of me, and washed it clean. I read and re-read these parts, and began to figure myself out.

The first night I started reading, I carefully flipped the pages, half in shock that someone actually felt the same way I had all of my teenage life, and half relieved at sharing such an understanding of my life with cystic fibrosis. I read word after word feeling a range of pain, comfort, more pain, and finally the healing that ran through me. I cried. I sniffled. I made noises that don't come from a weep. No, these were full-on sobs that could only come from a 16-year-old pubescent girl.

After it became too much, I pressed the sleep button on my clock radio to listen to the gentle voice of David Allen Boucher on Bed-Time Magic 106.7, and heard the familiar beat of Nana's song. The day Nana died, our whole family surrounded her. As she took her last breath, the room fell silent except for the radio, which I only noticed at that point. The song, "You'll Be in My Heart," by Phil Collins played. Soon after her death, the song came on whenever our family was going through something difficult. We called Nana, "The DJ in the Sky," and tonight she flew down to Boston, took the reins from David Allen Boucher, and was here with me: "Come, stop your crying it will be alright, just take my hand, hold it tight. I will protect you from all around you. I will be here don't you cry."

I wished I could pluck the pain I felt and hand it over for Mike to feel, with a deep understanding that only comes with love. I had cried about being alone. Now, so unexpectedly, at such a meaningful time, here she was, and I didn't feel so alone. I cried even harder, but this time I was in awe.

"Thank you," I whispered.

The next day, Mike had come over. I begged him not to leave, afraid of what feelings would crop up after tonight's reading, afraid of facing my biggest fears and subconscious pain. He said goodnight with a kiss, tucked me in, and turned off the light. Watching his car turn the corner, I flicked on the light, took out my pink pen, and continued reading. This time, my tears were light, and the book became more and more positive and healing.

I called him and blurted out, "There was a reason I didn't want you to leave."

I explained my epiphany from the night before. He told me that he was always here for me, and I told him I wanted him to read the book. After Mike promised he would read it as soon as I was done, I went to sleep.

I finished the book, and handed it over to him the Friday before I left for Cape Cod with my family and best friend. I called him Saturday night, and he told me he was almost through the book. We didn't go any deeper than that. Later, while my friend fought with her boyfriend over the phone, I texted Mike about the book.

"Rly tho, how did you lyke it?" I tapped.

"I cried."

I choked up, and turned to the side of my bed, replying, "You did?"

"Twice…"

I didn't realize the meaning of these tears until the following Monday.

He hands me the faded yellow book.

"I have some questions," he says.

"Okay."

After a series of simple questions about treatments, pills, and diets, he pauses and takes a breath.

"What is progressive? And is that what yours is?"

I swallow.

"Yes… it means it only gets worse."

I collapse into his arms and bury my face in his shoulder. I feel his warm tears on my shirt.

"What else? Throw it at me." I say.

"I don't know if I can."

He kisses me, my forehead, my cheeks, my tears, my lips.

"I love you so much," I say.

"I have a question about your underline… umm… something you double underlined, hold on I wrote a note…" he talks while flipping through the book.

He shows me the page, marked with his green pen. *"And it is so hard to be positive when you not only face fears but face them alone."* I squint at the green words in his scratchy hand-writing, "no you don't."

"You don't have to face them alone, babe," he says, not breaking eye contact. "You don't have to face them alone."

I hug him. I squeeze and cry and all of my pain, all of my loneliness pour into this boy. I know he feels everything I have felt. It feels like a flame is lit, filled with a sense of understanding, of well-being, a connection like no other, as if two souls have merged into one.

"I love you so much," I cry, the most meaningful and heartfelt I love you had said up until that point, at the ripe old age of 16.

He hugs me just as hard. It feels like an open door letting in a draft has finally been closed and replaced with a warm fire. We talk more about my condition, about hope for the future, where he would be by my side. I'm lying on his chest and listening to his heartbeat.

"Ya know what?" he asks.

"Mhm?" I hum.

"When I think about other couples, just any other couple, who just had life handed down to them I feel like… me and you… we both have to face stuff."

He pauses and I gave his hand a squeeze.

"That makes us special," he kisses my forehead.

"We are special."

* * *

Now, two years later, I sit in my green shag butterfly chair, staring into his green eyes on the other side of the computer screen hundreds of miles away, with words in my throat but nothing to say.

"I… I'm sorry… I just needed to talk to someone. Maybe I shouldn't have IMed you."

"No, Lau, it's good to see you. What's up?"

I tell him how much it sucks being at home sick, and leave the part about Faith out. I don't tell him I miss him, or that I wish he were here to go through it with me, to write in green pen next to the words in my book. The flame isn't burning any more.

"I know," is all he can say.

I take a moment to just look at him, taking a breath to speak before thinking better of it.

"So, I, I guess I'll see you around during winter break?" I say.

"Yeah," he says. "Maybe you will."

I close my laptop and bang my head on my desk. That was so stupid. What did I expect him to say? He can't do anything to face my fears with me, he was relieved of those duties the day he dropped me off at my house in his mini-van and drove off to California. This isn't his battle. It's mine. Before I can expect any one person to share the burden on my shoulders, I have to come to terms with it on my own. I open up iTunes and scroll down the artists until I get to "P." I find Phil Collins, and click on "You'll Be in My Heart."

Let Them Be an Asshole
Once in a While

"I hate you."

"You don't understand"

"Leave me alone."

"Go away!"

"YOU suck!"

Eye rolling.

Door slamming.

Sound familiar? I have said and done every one of these to my parents, usually when I was feeling my worst. See, as a child (and even as an adult), you're able to take your frustrations out on your parents, because you know that at the end of the day, they're still going to love you, take care of you, and forgive you. My parents could always tell when I wasn't feeling well because I started acting like the devil herself.

* * *

I'm 8 years old, and my dad is blessed with the daunting task of waking me up in the morning, cooking me breakfast, and begging me to do my treatments

He knocks gently on my door, whispering that I need to wake up.

"Five more minutes," I plead, and roll over to go back to sleep.

Soon, I hear a knock again, and the rage starts.

"How dare he expect that I wake up! I'm so tired!"

I mumble my way out of bed, wrapping my fleece blanket around my back and up over my head, galumph down the stairs, and sit at the dinner table. I slip my hand out of my blanket cape to rip off pieces of the raisin bagel, toasted with butter, that Dad has ready on the table.

I grump about my morning. He is not deterred.

"Treatment Time!" he sings.

Some days, I comply. Today, like most days, I barter, and offer compromises like, "what if I do it when I get home from school?" or, "I promise, promise if you just let me skip today I'll never ask you to skip it again." He's heard it all. Some days I yell, tell him he's stupid and I don't *want* to do that *stupid* thing. Other days, I stomp up the stairs and hide. But his patience prevails.

"Lauren," he says, "you know I'm only making you do this because I love you and don't want you to get sick."

It was a line he and my mom used often, and today it works. I dramatically whip The Vest around my back and shove my arms through the arm holes, fumbling with the buckles and grunting when they don't line up right. Once I've squeezed the vial of medicine into the cup, I jam the nebulizer into my mouth, biting down on the mouthpiece so hard the plastic distorts. I inhale and huff out the mist of my medication, watching the cloud blow out like a boiling tea kettle.

* * *

As I got older, the frustrations took less obvious forms. One day in particular stands out when my parents bore the brunt of my wrath, horns growing out of the side of my head, my tail whipping back and forth behind me. The previous night, I lay tossing and turning. My PICC line, where medicine gets delivered into my arm, is in serious need of a dressing change. It is beginning to get itchy, uncomfortable, and each time I roll into a position, my arm where it sits feels heavy, restless, and sore.

Finally, around 2AM, the gentle hum of the IV pump lulls me to sleep.

2:30AM: the 5-note alarm of my IV pump begins. I wait for a nurse to come.

I hear commotion outside, feet running into the room next to me. A code. In hospital speak, that means all hands on deck, for the patient next door, not for me. I lay staring at the ceiling, my eyelids heavy, but wide open. The five notes begin echoing in my head, "Beep beep beep… beep beep… Beep beep beep… beep beep." Adrenaline coursing through my veins, I try to let the gentle beeps lull me back to sleep, but they turn into a cacophony of deafening bells, swirling around my head. Usually, a nurse will peak her head in to unhook me from the IV pole; it feels like the alarm has been going off for an hour with no nurse in sight. I reach to the side of my bed, wincing at the soreness in my arm, and press the call bell haphazardly, burying my head into my pillow. At 3:00AM the tears start as I groan my way up to look at the machine. I press a button that looks like it will make the alarm stop, and it does. Silence. My teeth unclench, I breathe, stretch, and roll over to shut my eyes.

Until 3:05AM, when it starts again. I slam my head into the pillow and roar, gritting my teeth and gripping my head. I lay there, pissed off, staring at the ceiling, panting. Until finally, at 3:30AM, the nurse rushes in and sees me wide-eyed.

"Sorry…" she huffs, hurrying to disconnect the tubes of my medication, and silences the alarm for good.

I lay awake until 4:30AM, trying to tell my body to calm the fuck down, almost laughing at how absurd it is that I'm still awake. At 6:00AM, my nurse comes in for the next medication infusion, and a doctor slips in behind her. I open my eyes to give the nurse my arm.

"Oh, you're awake!" the doctor exclaims. "Mind if I have a listen?"

I sit up groggily, adjust my shirt, and proceed to inhale and exhale while he places his cold stethoscope on my back. He goes through his laundry list of questions and I answer them in monotone. Then he's finally done.

"Have a good day, Lauren!" he waves, letting the door slam behind him.

I flop onto my pillow and breathe a heavy sigh, rubbing my eyes. By 7:00AM, my nurse is back, and I'm awake for the rest of the day.

That afternoon, my parents come in with a homemade meal. I bark orders to have them heat up the food, and snap at my mom when she asks about my medication schedule.

"I don't KNOW mom, God… would you just RELAX?!"

But it isn't her I'm mad at. I'm mad because I got woken up at 2:30AM by machines beeping. I'm mad because I feel like crap, but I'm not quite sick enough that the 6:00AM doctors think I need my rest. I'm mad because my friends have stopped coming to visit. I'm mad that I'm missing out on everything going on at school. I'm mad because my lungs are aching, and I'm so. Fucking. Tired.

Mom and Dad don't know this. All they know is they're dealing with a very crabby daughter, who is in desperate need of something, and it's not them fussing over her. They get it. They quickly eat their dinner with me.

"Lau," Mom says, "why don't you use this time to take a nap?"

Her and Dad get up and quietly shut the door to go for a walk downstairs.

Put yourself in that room that night, alarms going off beyond your control. And just when you experience a small degree of relaxation, they start again. That's what it's like to have a chronic illness. Alarms going off without much warning, and often times it feels impossible to shut them off. This leaves you frustrated, exhausted, and undoubtedly grumpy when they keep you up all night. There have been days when my mom would question why I was acting so crabby, and sometimes, I couldn't put my finger on it.

But when I think back to that night of alarms, I realize what it was: I get grumpy when I feel out of control, and sometimes I just need someone to direct that negative energy towards, even if it's misdirected, and unfair. My parents always understood and never stayed mad because at the end of the day, they loved me, even when I used them as my punching bag.

As a kid, you're so full of these emotions you haven't yet learned how to master, control, or understand. I can guarantee that your child will get mad at you, say mean things, and be grumpy more than a few times in your life. As a parent, the gift you can give them is to understand they're not doing this because they hate you, don't want to take care of themselves anymore, or because you've done anything wrong. Nine times out of ten, it's because they need something, and you, as the parent, have the exciting task of understanding what that is.

For my dad, he knew I needed some food in the morning to get me going.

He knew doing my treatments and clearing out my lungs would make me feel a little bit better, so he dealt with the grunting and the fighting. And some days, he knew what I needed was to go back to bed, because he heard me up coughing all night. Most days, after I finished my treatments, and beat him in a game or two of Uno, I was back to my happy-go-lucky self. And some days I stayed grumpy, and that was a sure sign something was brewing in my lungs. Until you learn to read your child, you may misinterpret their rebellion as something it's not. When you accept it, and love them despite it, they're able to figure it out on their own.

Remember when your kid was a baby? They would cry and cry until they got what they truly needed at the time. It would be crazy to simply tell them to stop crying without giving them that bottle, that diaper change, or putting them down for that nap. Us chronically ill kids are much the same. We grump around and sometimes we don't know why. Our parents help to bridge that gap, as we're still learning to take care of ourselves.

Now, none of this is to say that allowing your kid to act like a brat is okay, but if you force them to hold in their anger, you'll never be able to understand what it is they truly need. As I got older, I finally understood I was being a little irrational, and would apologize to my undeserving parents, and thank them for letting me get it out. And even if your kid doesn't have the guilt that I have, they sometimes just need to be a jerk for no reason, and it's okay to let them once in a while.

How to Deal with the D Word

This topic scares the shit out of people, so I'm going to take your hand and walk you through it, like in a haunted house except there won't be any zombies, and I'll warn you when the scary clowns are about to appear. So, without further adieu it's time to talk about the D word. It's not DIRT, and it's not DIRTY, and it's not every other poo-oriented D word that first came to mind.

It's death.

It's the difficult conversation that will inevitably come. And if the conversation isn't about death, it will be a similarly difficult conversation, about the less glamorous sides of our disability: being different, feeling limited, getting made fun of, etc.

We humans aren't too keen on talking about death, I've noticed. The super sad books and online articles you'll find do a clever little dance around death, and they go to both extremes:

1) They pretend like it's not going to happen, or try to give you hope that *if only* you do this, this, and this, it can be avoided,

OR

2) It's talked about in a *super sad* way, because the article or book is about someone who died. And that is never *not* sad. It's telling you to hold

your children tight, because this woman you don't know lost hers, and the next thing you know your bed is covered in tissues—because life is just so sad and you feel so sad for every living thing that has ever met its maker.

But no one tells it like it is. Where is the in between? Where are the conversations about talking to your kids about their own mortality? Going one step further, where are the conversations about people ever being comfortable with the idea of *their own* mortality? For now, I'll keep referring to it as the D word (and you can insert whichever D word makes you giggle enough as to not feel super upset by this subject). Okay? Are we ready?

Someone approached me once, and asked if I would talk to a teenager with cf. She was 16-years-old, and her mother never had the D Word talk with her (no, not that D word...). And guess what? One of her classmates told her she was going to D word, and her poor mom didn't know what to do. I thought long and hard about whether talking to me would do anything to help her cope with the gigantic subject of her own mortality, and ultimately declined because: I do not have a PhD in psychology, and there was nothing I could say to make that situation okay. This was a deeply rooted issue. The daughter was probably pretty sad that she might D word from cf, but the deeper issue was that she was PISSED that her mom, the person she trusted most, wasn't the one to fill her in on that small detail.

I talked to her mom and gave her the hard truth.

"This is a tough conversation that *has* come from you, not a random college kid on the internet."

As the parent, you are the keeper of the big secret, and you bear the responsibility of conveying that secret in the best way possible when the time is right, and hopefully before their bully jerk friends do (don't worry, I'll tell you how my mom did it and why she kicks ass).

My mom was a critical care nurse for 22 years. She came home and literally smelled like D word. I would sit on the couch as she swung open the creaking door after a 12-hour shift. Some days, she ran upstairs to shower because it was a rough day. I still remember the smell wafting past the kitchen table. It was stale, but mixed with the scent of mom's perfume, with her caring and compassion.

Conversations around the dinner table were frank, and I quickly learned to be okay with blood and guts, and people who were D wording, while eating my spaghetti and meatballs.

Our family was a young one in our neighborhood, so it seemed like our neighbors were always D wording. Having a nurse in the neighborhood meant my mom often found herself preparing the family for hospice, and comforting them when their loved one finally D worded. She seemed to go to more funerals than most. In fact, when Mom went to a medium, the medium told her she saw something like the Verizon commercial, where the guy is standing there with thousands of people behind him saying, "Can you hear me now? GOOD!"

Death surrounded her, but it wasn't because she was one of those people who hugged you extra tight and knew just the right thing to say, it was because she developed a healthy relationship with it, when most people would shy away from it, and avoid it at all costs.

When Mom was working as a critical care nurse she had two patients on the floor who were husband and wife. They were both heading towards the end. One day, the wife told my mom she wanted to see her husband. Because they were both so sick, they weren't allowed to leave their room, let alone go into another sick patient's room. But, rules weren't something you followed when you were about to D word. So, in the middle of the night, my mom wheeled the wife down the hall to see her husband. They sat next to each other holding hands and gazing into each other's eyes. My mom snuck out to give them some privacy, and then sneakily wheeled the wife back to her room and helped her into bed. The next day, the husband passed away, and shortly after, so did the wife.

Of course, for my mom the D word was sad. But knowing it was near was also a time to do what needed to be done, to live out your final wishes, and embrace your time on Earth. That's what she instilled in me. She was always wheeling me down the metaphorical hall to see my metaphorical husband, doing the things that needed to be done when your life is gonna be shorter than the average person.

The first time I was admitted to the hospital, I became friends with a D wording teenager named Hector. At the time, I didn't know he was going to D word. I knew he graduated early, but he told little 7-year-old me it was because he was so smart. I knew he was voted Prom King, but that was no surprise because he charmed every patient, nurse, and Child Life Specialist on 9-East. I also knew he had an 8-inch scar on the front of his chest from heart surgery, and that doctors spent a lot of time outside his door whispering to his mother, and that she spent a lot of time walking up and down the halls after those conversations.

To me, Hector was just someone doing the things he needed to do in his life. I thought it was cool that he graduated early, and that he was planning a big vacation to Hawaii for when he got out of the hospital. I thought that's just what sick kids in the hospital do, they live big when they aren't there. I didn't know then that kids like Hector had developed an intricate understanding of their own mortality.

Remember the report I did in 5th grade on cystic fibrosis? Since Google wasn't the magic that it is today, we actually used books to do our research. My mom gave me her book all about cf, written for adults. Oops. The first sentence was, "Cystic Fibrosis is a chronic, progressive, life-threatening illness that primarily affects the lungs and digestive system. There is no cure." Uh…

I took the book to my mom.

"What does that mean?" I asked.

"Well…" she said. "It means that some day, cf could eventually kill you. But, you know what? You or I could get hit by a bus tomorrow. People can D word giving birth, of a heart attack, or in a car accident. That is why we do Great Strides walks to raise money for cf, and why it's so important that we take care of you."

Surprisingly, this was an acceptable answer and I went on with my day. I wasn't particularly upset by this, because I, frankly, thought I was invincible and that D word thing happened to everyone else, not me.

But I kept this knowledge, and distinctly remember telling my classmates a year later, "I'm going to D word when I'm like 30!" (Dance!? Doo-Doo!? Dick around?!), as if this was something to brag about! I distinctly remember that moment, because I was beginning to come to terms with it, and I wanted people to know that it's normal, it's okay, and I was aware of it. So that no one could do what that 16-year-old's classmates did. I owned it. Kids with chronic illnesses do some weird shit, but to me, *that* was my normal. I never knew a time when I would live to be 100, because the one time I thought about my own mortality, I realized that NONE of it was a given.

It wasn't until I actually faced death myself that it began to upset me, and I started to get freaked out at the thought of it. It was a few years after the D word talk that the Great Blood Geyser of 2005 happened. While it was a big wake up call for taking care of myself, it was also my first personal introduction to the D word.

Once the doctors had left us alone, after telling me I was in shock and needed a blood transfusion, my mom held my hand and I squeezed it like I always did.

"Mom, am I going to D word?" I asked.

"The doctors are going to take care of you," she said. "And I'm going to be right by your side, okay?"

The truth is, I probably wasn't going to D word. But she didn't know, all she knew was that she was going to love me and hold me and be right there.

From that point on, whenever I felt my breathing getting more labored, or fevers knocked me down, or I watched my weight on the scale dip dangerously low, I got scared. More than anything, my future scared the hell out of me, but Mom was there to support and validate that fear. At the same time, she was there bringing me back to the present, counting my blessings on each of my fingers with me, and making sure I didn't forget how to laugh when things got rough. Even though she let me be sad, she never missed an opportunity to remind me to enjoy what we have.

That night, the nurse told us the blood I received had come from Tom Brady, who was currently playing in the Super Bowl (as if it said his name right on the pint bag). I chose to believe it. And even in the midst of the fear, my mom and I laughed about it, because being in the present moment, being pumped up with Sexy Tom Brady's blood, is where we needed to be.

The point is, my mother accepted, from a very early age, that her daughter *might* have a short life. Now, did she do this with a smile on her face? Absolutely not (that would be weird). Did she ever break down and cry because of it? Of course. But she accepted it, and that informed the way she allowed me to live my life.

I know instinctively that my shortened life can only be a catalyst for living it well, enjoying each of the moments I used to take for granted by wishing for better days, counting everything in my life I wanted but didn't yet have. I think about Faith, about how badly I just wanted to wade in that deep snow, and about the question I asked my mom that night in the emergency room, just before I received a blood transfusion.

"Am I going to die?"

The answer is yes. We all are, some day. We sick kids may have a deeper appreciation for how soon it *could* be, but it's something we all know deep down. We think we have enough time to procrastinate living, but there is no excuse. In fact, having an illness like mine works the opposite way: it's an excuse *not* to procrastinate, to pay attention to what is important, and to learn quickly what it means to appreciate life.

The most common thing I hear from parents who Google their child's illness is that the online world is too scary. And I mean… of course nothing about knowing people have died or gotten really sick from your child's illness is comforting. But what didn't come with those scary online stories was the question, "so what are we going to do with this information?" Cry about it, yes, you're allowed to do that for as long as you need to. After that comes the choice: Will you use the fact that life isn't a given as a catalyst to live life with purpose? Or will you let it put the brakes on living a good life?

Let Them Learn the Hard Way

Fridays in high school are payday, so after school I hop in my car and drive down to Peaceful Meadows, which, contrary to what it sounds like, is not a nursing home but an ice cream shop plopped down on a working dairy farm.

High school girls skip out of their cars, walk through the back room that reeks of sour milk and cow shit, and carefully flip through the pile of checks tucked into the safe. We open them there, scanning through the taxes and deductions to find out how much we can spend this weekend at the mall, or tuck into our savings accounts for whatever adventure we'll go on next summer. Today, our manager is on her break, so I grab a spoonful of chocolate ice cream on the way out, lean against the ice cream freezers, and commiserate with the girls who have to work tonight.

It's a typical check pick-up, except today my check has some overtime on it, so instead of turning right to go home, I turn left to go to Wendy's to grab some chicken nuggets. And a Frosty. Oh, and there's construction on Route 18 right outside the farm, which means the lane closest to me is filled with cars idling, their drivers' elbows rested on their doors, their hands holding frustrated heads.

Having had my license for just over a year, and inheriting the "defensive driving" techniques of my mom (which really means I wait way too long to take turns, and slam on my brakes at inopportune times, like when someone is driving by me on the other side of the road), I am trying to trust in my car a bit more. This means I didn't need a three point turn to get into a parking spot any more, and I use my rearview mirror to back up the car around my dad's in the driveway. And today, this means that, in typical Boston driver fashion, I'll inch into oncoming traffic to wait for an opportunity to go left. To my right is a large F150, blocking any view of the lane I need to be in.

Cars are honking, startling the cows in the pasture across the street.

"Does that mean I should go?"

I hesitate, take a breath, close my eyes, and gun it—right into a car zipping by. She swerves and I feel the jolt of my car against hers. *Shit.* I pull over. She gets out. Relief washes over me when I realize it's a teacher from the high school, but quickly whooshes away when I see the annoyed look on her face, the one that tells me she isn't going to give me the forgiveness I was looking for. We do what you do when you get in an accident, exchange information and all that. Then I get in my car, completely shaken and on the verge of tears at my own stupidity, and vow never to take a left turn again.

Of course, my vow is broken when I take a left into Wendy's and cry into my chicken nuggets. But, from that day forward every left turn I take is with hesitation, checking left and right, and left and right, and left and right one more time just to be sure Mrs. Pickett isn't zipping by. That one accident may have avoided another accident, because if I had zoomed left without looking right, and nothing bad happened, maybe I would have risked it again, and another time, until maybe it was a person crossing the street, unprotected by the shell of their Mazda. As shaken as I was, I learned a lesson that day, and it stuck with me for many years after, even if it meant I drove like a grandma.

Life's a bit like that, isn't it? It's a series of moments that teach you how you'll live your life going forward. Sometimes, you'll decide the consequences were bearable the first time, and maybe you'll make the same mistake again, get in another accident. Sometimes you might brush it off as a fluke, an unfortunate side effect of all the random factors of the moment: The Ford F150 blocking the view, the construction on the road. But sometimes, the moment is so powerful you're forced to make a change. Sometimes.

One of the hardest things as a parent is accepting there are moments that teach your child to make a change in the actions they take for their own health, and also moments that teach your child to make a change in the way they live their life. And those true life-altering moments tend to be immensely painful for the whole family. Lessons learned the hard way are often the most impactful, which sounds morbid, but when you look back, there's an odd degree of thankfulness for it. That's not to say you should let your kid go off the deep end before they can swim; you can't force these moments. But when they happen, as hard as it is while it's happening, as much as it seems nothing good will come of it, if they get to the other side with the help of your love, they will be changed.

What Happens When You Eat the Poop

During the last few days I'm home that first fall in college, with my PICC line, having severe FOMO, secondary heart-break, and a major case of being a giant asshole, I'm asleep on the couch only to be rudely awoken.

"MEKA!" I hear my mom screaming at my dog. "YOU DON'T EAT YOUR OWN POOP!"

Meka comes running into the house licking her chops. Dad rushes downstairs, asking what Mom is screaming about.

"The damn dog's eating her shit again!"

He waves her off and shrugs.

"Poopsicles. She just likes Poopsicles!"

I cover my face with the blanket and suppress a laugh.

Mom, frustrated with our poop-breathed dog, plops down on the couch next to me.

I open one eye.

"Maybe it's normal?"

"Whatever it is, it's gross," she sighs.

After the great poo incident I'm wide awake, so I boot up my laptop, open up Google, and type, "Why do dogs eat their own poop?"

"Well," I motion toward the screen, "It's normal! And dogs do it for a number of reasons. They might be bored, or stressed, or lacking some vitamins."

"Huh…" Mom considers.

I knew we'd been busy since I came home from school. I was hardly ever playing with her, and Mom and Dad sure weren't going to take her for walks because she pulled on the leash so much. I fancied myself a dog trainer, and she listened to my commands. But she knew she could get away with pouncing on the neighbor's Pekinese, and sniffing out the neighbor's dachshund when Mom and Dad were in charge, so they enjoyed their walks sans Meka.

Humans think it's gross that dogs eat poop, but all dogs do it at some point in their life, even if they aren't caught. Meka especially liked to chomp into the horse manure at the farm down the street where we sometimes took her for walks. But the truth is, we all go through a time in our life where we eat shit—where we can't stand the stress, the worry, the pain, and we shut down, and do things we never thought we would.

Just like I've grown accustomed to the daily medications and treatments, I've grown accustomed to the uncertainty, the fear, and the grip cf has on my body, whether I like it or not. This isn't easy, by any means, but resiliency takes over. Just like it eventually takes over for everyone. Yes, you can cry in the backseat of your car, but eventually you gotta pack your frog printed pajamas and get through it.

Living a resilient life isn't about having the strength to face every single obstacle. It's a never ending course that ebbs and flows, with peaks and valleys, a landscape of rolling hills. Some days, you look the challenges square in the eye and say, "I've got this." And other days, you feel like you don't have it in you to go on. You eat the shit. Gobble it right up without gagging, and let the negativity, self-doubt, and fear overcome you.

A few days after watching Meka eat shit, I move back into college—and eat my own four-course meal of shit. One night, I text my high school sweetheart: "When I go to bed… sometimes I think it'd be so great if I didn't wake up. Not that I am going to kill myself or anything, but it would just be so nice if I didn't wake up." Overwhelmed with lungs that sucked air like breathing through a straw, and faced with the foreboding reality that, although my family is there for me, in the moments when the lights are out and I'm alone with my thoughts, I know I am the one who has to deal with

WHAT HAPPENS WHEN YOU EAT THE POOP

the shit. I feel alone with the mountain of my future. I doubt I have the strength to come to terms with all the things I thought I had grown accustomed to, I swallow every last bit of shitty thought that crosses my mind: that I'm not strong enough, not trying hard enough, and worst of all, that no one will love me enough to bring out the resiliency that lay dormant within me.

When I look back on that moment, at the lowest point in my life, I see a person I don't recognize. I see a dog eating shit. Even though we thought it was so crazy that our dog would do something so gross, we learned that it was normal. It was a natural response to stress. We all do it. We all look back and may feel weak for letting ourselves sink so low, but it's normal. It isn't shameful, and sometimes we need to let ourselves be sad in order to awaken our true strength. (NOTE: Being suicidal is *not* something that's in the day to day sadness. When it progresses to this point, there are resources, counselors, hotlines, and people to talk to. In fact, the person I texted encouraged me to do just that).

I struggle when it comes to whether or not to share these types of stories, but it would be unfair for me to shrug it off and act like getting to a point of acceptance was easy, especially for people who look at me and think, "Crap, life really sucks for me right now... am I doing something wrong that I'm not as cheery as Lauren seems to be?"

Just as social media often only shows the positive moments, the one good family photo out of ten where each child is looking the other way, crying, and appears as a blur across the screen, we often only ever see a glimpse of resiliency and acceptance—after they've appeared. We see the person celebrating at the top of the mountain, but we don't see the sweat and the sore legs it took to get there, the equipment guiding them up, the people supporting them, or the inner dialogue when they wanted to give up.

Some take longer than others to get to a point of acceptance, especially when depression takes over, but soon enough, with the right combination of support, self-determination, and reflection, it appears and puts your life into perspective. Eventually, I saw that when I don't have a choice or a means to control the situation, I can either wallow in self-pity, or I can adapt and stop looking at the things that are missing, and instead at the people, the blessings, and the simple experiences that have been there all along. Here I was worrying that no one would love me, when I had a mountain of love surrounding me in my family.

As the semester draws to a close, I stop looking everywhere for a boyfriend, for a crutch to hold onto, and dive head first into my group of new friends, my school work, and get to work on loving myself. That winter, I get to run through unspoiled, waist deep snow to slide down the tall, steep Donahue Hill on Stonehill's campus, perched on a tray stolen from the cafeteria—and it hits me. This is what I wanted so badly that week in the hospital before I saw my life flash before my eyes. I just wanted to be in the present moment, in waist deep snow, and enjoy it.

The Sketchy Motel

A couple months after I eat the shit, I plan a day trip to Killington Mountain in Vermont to ski with two friends from Stonehill. Our group is me, the young, petite girl who has made the trek up to Killington a half dozen times; Kind Kyle, the snowboarder who is dating a girl back at his high-school; and Ryan, the cool new friend everyone makes in college.

I love the three and a half hour drive up through the mountains, snaking through unplowed roads without white lines etched between lanes. There's something about the way the mountain range makes foreboding shadows in the morning light that gets my adrenaline rushing to ski one of the largest mountains in New England.

We spend the three-hour drive playing our favorite songs on our iPods, until they die and the radio gives way to static in the deep valleys of the white mountains. I'm pumped that Kyle loves country music just as much as I do, and tease that I don't need girl friends when he likes Taylor Swift and Justin Bieber so much.

When it isn't my turn to drive, I rest my head against the window and take in all of the scenery: the tall evergreens, the walls of ice latched to boulders that had been blasted to make this road through the mountains, the green signs coated in salt from the road. I laugh, and tell the guys about how my mom is always yelling at my dad to keep his eyes on the road on drives like these. His head always swivels in every direction, pointing out the campgrounds and mountain passes he had hiked when he was a kid. To myself, I muse about how much he appreciates in the scenery, the stories held tight in the places he came to love, and how by his example, my head is nearly turning 360 degrees to take it all in—on this drive and in life.

It isn't weird that I'm with two guys. Growing up with two brothers, it's always been my natural habitat. All through high school, I surrounded myself with guy friends, not wanting the drama that inevitably came with girls. So I found my few close ladies, but when it's time for adventure, I always know the guys won't disappoint.

The day rewards us with snow that never stops, piling up on our laps on the long chairlift ride. Kyle and I race through the powdery snow, and I tell him stories about each of the trails we go down, like the time I lost my brothers and spent the afternoon cruising the slopes alone. Or the time we raced down the longest, windiest green trail and I thought I might fly off my skis from the speed. Or the time my cousin skied off the trails into the woods, and got to the bottom after the lifts had stopped running, miles away from the lot where he had parked his car.

This is another moment I promise myself I won't take for granted. In the moments when our laughing dies down, giving way to the squeaking of the chairlift and the swishing of skis on the trails below, I let my mind wander back to that hospital room in 2005, watching the snow pile up in between the buildings, and take a breath.

Stopping for waffles, we talk to some ski patrol guys about the weather.

"Yeah, this stuff is gonna dump all night! I hope you're not driving home in this!"

We decide instantly. Instead of packing up our ski bags and inching home on the slippery roads, I call my brother Dave to get the name of the motel he's crashed in plenty of nights, after a day of chasing powder.

"It's not the nicest motel, a little sketchy… the guy lives in the trailer out back, but it's like sixty bucks for the night. Just don't tell them how many people are staying, he'll charge you extra."

Make it an adventure.

After we dig out our car and freeze our noses and finger tips, we stop for toothbrushes, and use the GPS to navigate to the motel, marked by bears flanking the front doors. Kyle waits in the car. Ryan and I go in to do our best impression of a couple staying the night, holding mittens while traipsing through the front door, Ryan carefully opening it for me.

We ask the burly man, his long gray beard resting on his beer belly, for a room for the night. He grunts, shuffles out back, drops a key on the counter, and writes a receipt on a tiny piece of paper.

"There's a hot tub out back by my trailer if you're interested. See you in the mawnin'."

I skip out with the keys, and we clamber through the snow to check out the hot tub. We see a small tub, enough for two intimately related people, covered in about a foot of snow next to an old metal trailer. I die laughing, remembering my brother's warning. Sketchy indeed.

"Scratch the hot tub."

We unload our ski boots so they will stay warm for another day of skiing tomorrow and unlock the door, peering inside the musty room to find two worn out beds.

We're exhausted, and Kyle's phone keeps buzzing. His girlfriend. From what I can tell, they're in the middle of breaking up.

"Kyle," I say, "you can't dump her in a text message."

So he picks up the phone and steps outside, while I discover a pack of cards right next to the Bible in the bedside table. Ryan and I play cards on the bed. This is the third time they have broken up this year, and this time she's mad that he's staying over with another girl. What she doesn't know is that this girl's busy worrying, while shuffling the deck and dealing the cards, that she doesn't have her nighttime medicine, or her vest and nebulizers for the morning, and that she isn't even considering Kind Kyle as a romantic option. Not to mention, the must is starting to settle in her lungs.

Kyle swings open the door.

"Well, it's over."

I console him and he laughs.

"I'm just happy to be done with her. It was getting a little ridiculous."

I'm careful about the bed I choose to sleep in. Ryan is just a cool friend, so I choose newly-single-as-of-an-hour-ago Kyle, and promise I won't kick him in my sleep. I scooch over so we aren't too close and say goodnight to the boys.

In the middle of the night, I'm shivering—I don't think the heater is working at all. I wake myself up with a few irritated coughs, and feel Kyle's arm pull me in close and bring the covers up over my shoulders. I let myself fall into him, keeping my eyes closed—hoping I can hide how cozy it feels, and how nervous I am.

Ocean Waves

After a month or so of avoiding Kyle, and even dating other people, I finally admit I'm falling for him. And when word gets around to his ex-girlfriend, we quickly hear from her sister. She sends Kyle a message, as dramatic high school girls do, and in so few words tells him she cannot believe he is with a dying girl. When he shows me the message, I shrug.

"Just give 'em something to talk about," I say.

This is one of those fights not worth fighting.

In a matter of months, the guy who snuggled with me during my cough attack becomes more than just my ski buddy. In the morning, he meets me for breakfast. After class, reminds me to take my pills, and makes the trek back to my dorm room on the days I run out of the stash in my purse. He sits on my bed and reads his Biology text book while I do my vest, and some days we meet outside of our dorm to go for a run around campus. He never flinches at the piles of pill bottles on my desk, or the shaking coughs that sometimes rattle my body. So on the day we are going about our usual, "I like you… a lot," routine, and the other L word slips, I panic.

"I love you," he says in the gushy tone we were using that day.

"Shut up," I say. "No you don't."

And we don't bring it up again for a full month. At that time, I knew he couldn't love me. He hadn't yet felt what I felt, what my parents felt, when we thought about the future with cystic fibrosis. He had never seen me at my sickest, nor did he truly understand that loving me came with an unfair burden. How could he even know what love is?

Shortly after I tell him to, "shut up," I have a doctor's appointment. It's my first appointment after the great shit eating incident, and I'm anxious to see how my lung function has changed since then. I inhale and exhale, draw a deep breath in, and blow out as much as I can into the tube that measures how my lungs are doing with the whole breathing thing. I see the number on the screen, barely improved from the last time I was here. My heart sinks. I think back to the book I read for my 5th grade report and can see those words: progressive, chronic, incurable. Before, those were words on paper, but the numbers in front of me are very real. I always knew this illness was life-threatening. I lived through near-death experiences. My friend died from this disease. But today, the numbers on the screen slap me across the face.

* * *

I'm 16, on summer vacation with my family in Dennis, Massachusetts. From my beach chair, I glance up from the book I'm reading to watch a group of little kids, the youngest girl in particular, who stands facing the ocean. I see what she sees: The usual Cape Cod water is murky but inviting, with the blue sky reflecting into the hazy waters it transforms into a welcoming greenish blue, as if emerald, sapphire, and tree bark were mixed together. However, a visitor from somewhere like the Caribbean might mistake it as unwelcoming, wondering what creatures are lurking under the dark water. Yesterday, the waves pounded the shore of the beach. Today, the low tide waves are calm, and trickle up to the shore like a baby bird peeking out from his nest, only to retreat back into safety, not yet ready for what the big world has to hold.

Maybe it's the memories I have along the shores of this beach, or maybe it's the fact that I had just sat along it with Mike the night before. Whatever it is, the nostalgia calms me in a way no human can. The little girl takes in the ocean with its waves that can gently pick her up, jumping over the waves that are tiny to me, but enormous to her. In her eyes, it's her new friend.

I see this beach as a scrapbook of my life, bringing about a new memory with each crash of the waves. I remember the friends, the cousins that swam with me in the water, their bright eyes squinting in the August sun. I see my little feet feeling the soft sand being carried back into the ocean with the undertow of the crashing wave. Then I see my feet grow, each year, returning to the ocean to stand in the wake of the waves. These growing feet that walk newer, wider, and longer paths between each time they return to the sea. The sea is and has always been forgiving, recognizing them as mine and mine alone, although these feet have found new exciting ground, and the body these feet support labors a bit more with each breath.

The small girl watches her older sister create a new game. She stands on the dry sand. The wave crashes and the girl prepares to run. The water chases her dancing feet and she giggles and screams, running at a runner's sprint so the ice cold water won't touch her feet. When the defeated water goes back to its nest, she follows it and stands in her original spot. Her sisters, cousins, and friends watch her live in the glory of beating the wave every time. Soon, they all join in on the game, running away from the chasing water only to return back for another thrill.

Gazing back into the ocean, I watch the waves rolling in. A larger one approaches, and the anticipation in the children's eyes grows to match its size. *Crash*, and they set off, marathon runners at the sound of the gun. A wall of them runs, screaming the five or so feet they have to escape from the oncoming water. I see the oldest ones standing, looking at the retreating water as if it were the last place finisher, proud that they beat the wave, with moments to spare.

Then I see the little sister facing me. She still has her swimmies around her arms, and is still running from the water. The water reaches her, pools around her ankles, and she keeps running until her little ankles are free from the water's shackles, laughing, screaming, and settling in with her peers. I smile, noting the excitement in her eyes—the deepest of all the children. She's so proud to have crossed the finish line, so much so that she doesn't even notice her soaked feet. Even though the little girl can never beat it, she keeps her composure and plays the game regardless, having the most fun.

I see myself in the little girl's eyes, the same sapphire emerald bark of the Cape Cod water. The waves keep coming back to me, and no matter how much I run away from them, they always touch my ankles. No matter how accomplished I become, no matter how many waves I jump over, no matter how old I am or how long the paths I walked are, the waves chase me and pool around my ankles nonetheless. Sure, running back to my towel would be a quick solution, but eventually the low tide will turn to high tide, and the waves will chase again. So I allow the inevitable tide to grab hold of my ankles, knowing that soon enough, the wave might retreat. And I'll beat it.

I have come to expect the returning of the tide, the ebb and flow of life with a chronic illness. And yet—like the little sister on the beach—I persist. Why are we so surprised when life throws difficulties at us? At our children? At our family? Why are we so hell-bent on making life so perfect, so easy, and so devoid of the moments that shape us into the people we are?

Until you begin to see challenges as opportunities, and to see open doors instead of roadblocks, you'll continue to be disappointed when life happens. I don't mean the life you wish for, I mean the life that is inevitable in all of its surprises. Between all the game winning home runs, life throws us curve balls. Some of us have to dodge those curve balls earlier in life than others. But some of us learn to catch them earlier, too. I call that acceptance.

* * *

That night, Kyle and I go for a walk around campus. I tell him how scared I am, seeing the trend chart of my lung function dipping so low, but I also tell him about the ebb and flow of life with cf. How at the same time I'm terrified for my future, I'm content with this moment right here. We walk hand in hand, and settle on a bench in the shadow of a streetlight.

"Kyle, are you sure you want to be with me?"

"Lauren, all I know is that I like being with you right now. Yes, it's scary, but when I think about you, I see someone who makes me laugh and enjoys life. How about we just enjoy *that*? I like being with you. You're the strongest person I know, and I want to enjoy every single minute I'm with you. That's all that matters."

I hug him, letting the silence get stuck under the street light. The waves are pooling around our ankles, but we can still splash in them.

Climb Your Own Hill

It's August and I'm running the Falmouth Road Race. Kind Kyle is by my side. To my right is the ocean, and up ahead the road curves to reveal a New England lighthouse, crisp white and black against a robin's egg blue sky. All around me feet pound the pavement, breaths huff up the hill. I look down at my shirt. Underneath the Cystic Fibrosis Foundation (CFF) logo are the words, written in T-shirt paint, "I have cf, So What?!"

It's been two years since I first told Kyle I loved him. I've been running consistently that whole time, with Kyle by my side. During this time, a drug that treats a small subset of the cf population, not including me, has been approved. I read stories of people who can breathe again, of people with cf saving money for retirement, and of parents crying because their kid has a future. My lung function hasn't dipped since my test two years ago. I haven't seen a hospital room for two years. As I round the corner onto the beach, I feel my legs get heavy and my lungs tighten up, gasping for breath in the thick August air, made worse by the beating sun. I start to walk.

"Let's go CFF!" someone calls out from the crowd.

I feel the strength come back. I look back from where I came, over the 17 hills I've climbed since Woods Hole, and I thank them for the strength they've given me to move forward.

Most of what I remember about my freshman year of college are the times the fire alarm went off. Usually, the diagnosis was microwave related: someone left their popcorn in for too long, someone tried to make Easy-Mac without water, or ramen noodles went unchecked and smoked out the dorm. Outside, people would exit Boland Hall in various levels of disarray. The, "I was fast asleep-ers," the, "I just had sex-ers," (and the resulting guests), and the, "I'm way too drunk for this-ers." At the beginning of the year, Kyle was always the one who was fast asleep, in his boxers, and he proudly paraded outside in his green bathrobe and slippers to talk about the latest drunk who set off the fire alarm, and to withstand our barrage of jests about his grandpa robe.

Once Kyle and I started dating, we came outside together to take in the scene. One night, (a waterless Easy-Mac night) our friend Tom was an, "I'm way too drunk for this-er." He plucked a cigarette from behind his ear to light up. I was also an, "I'm way too drunk for this-er," and had some thoughts about the cigarette he plucked from behind his ear.

"Tom!" I commanded. "Get that thing out of your mouth! *Whattaya wanna* kill ya'self?"

"BOMBA!" he exclaimed my nickname, like I was a long-lost friend. "Come here!"

He wrapped me up in a hug, holding out his cigarette to avoid burning my hair.

"But seriously, ya don't need that thing," I slapped it out of his hand.

"What the…"

The alarm stopped, cheers erupted on the lawn outside, and RA's ushered us into the building. Back inside the dorm, settling at the edge of his bed, I experienced Kyle's disappointed face for the first time—the way he rose his eyebrows, scrunched up his forehead, and pursed his lips as if they were a levy holding back the tide.

"What?" I questioned. "What is it?"

"What do you *think* it is, Lau?"

"Come on, you know I hate smokers!"

"It doesn't matter. He's our friend."

Had I been an, "I was fast asleep-er," I probably would have silently fumed to myself about how stupid our friend was, and politely stood away from the puff surrounding him, but I was Too. Drunk. For. This. And the fresh wound of my friend passing away was at the forefront of my drunken decisions. How could people take their life for granted when people were dying? How could someone do something so knowingly deadly? How could the people of the world be ruining their lungs when people like Faith could have used them?

During waterless Easy-Mac fire alarm night, having recently gained the maturity to take personal responsibility for whether or not I lived or died, it infuriated me when people hadn't drawn the same conclusions for their own lives. Kyle didn't even need to say it. The frustration I was feeling sounded a lot like how my parents felt every time I fought them to do my treatments, when I left pills untaken in the daily plastic pill organizer, and when I stayed out late when they knew I needed the rest. His raised eyebrows told me how they would probably feel about the state I was in right now. After all, even though I was at a point where I wasn't skipping out on medications… getting drunk probably wasn't putting my health at Priority #1.

Slapping the cigarette was unfair. We all draw our own conclusions. It takes life experience for it to click. Some get lucky and it clicks sooner rather than later. Others take the liberty to enjoy a smoke with their buddies, knowing they're filling their lungs with cancer, because that life is what matters to them. And that life matters to them because their life hasn't shown them otherwise. We are all personally responsible for whether we live or die in some respects, but we are also personally responsible to be imperfect, let life take precedence, and learn and adapt to the spectrum of health vs. life on our own, at our own pace, even when it looks destructive on the outside.

One of the hardest things I've had to come to terms with is that there's a limit to how much you shape any other person's life. After all, every one of us is human, so human that we make our own mistakes, fall down on the ground, and decide whether or not we'll get back up. Then, our human-ness even dictates whether or not we let ourselves make those mistakes again. And then our humanity takes us one step further, and lets us decide whether we will take anything away from that trip, whether we'll decide to look at the ground when we're walking instead of burying our noses in our phones, or whether we will find any deeper meaning or take any responsibility for it. What is most important is that we are surrounded by love and forgiveness for wanting to figure it out on our own.

Kyle and I come around the corner, preparing to approach the final hill, at the 7th mile. To my right is my family, my mom and dad out in front. I slow down and wrap my arms around them, their love giving me the strength to go on, like it has so many times before, but ultimately I'm the one who pulls my tired legs up the tall hill overlooking the water.

In Sickness and in Health

On July 3, 2015, I learned that a drug that would treat the underlying cause of my illness was approved by the FDA. Just a couple weeks later, I wait on hold with my pharmacy while driving home to my apartment outside of Boston.

The representative gets back on the line. This is it.

"Okay," she says nonchalantly, "your prior authorization has been accepted by the insurance company. When would you like us to ship it out?"

I hesitate, a wave of emotion stealing the words from my throat.

"Uh…" I stammer, "as soon as possible, please. I know you do this all day long, but you have no idea what this means to me. I have been waiting for this medication for ten years. Thank you."

I flip on my blinker and pull over. Resting my head against the steering wheel, I breathe in the moment, thinking back to the day I sat crying in the new room, watching the birds outside the window. I think about the waist deep snow, Faith's cackle in her hospital bed, that night I got Tom Brady's blood. The first person I call is my mom.

"Guess what's coming August 8th?"

"Oh my God! Lauren, this is so exciting. We've waited so long and now here it is. Are you freaking out?"

My whole body is shaking with excitement. I have the urge to get out of my car and dance, but decide to stick it out for the five minutes home. As soon as I open the door, I grab my shorts, sports bra, and tank top. After tying my running sneakers, I open the door and bound down my front steps and onto the street, my energy piercing the pavement. I run and run, even though it's hard to breathe in the humid July air, even though my feet start to throb, promising myself that from this moment on I won't take another breath for granted, regardless of how much easier those breaths will become.

I open the door and Kyle is just getting home from work.

"You're not gonna believe the news I just got!"

He picks me up and twirls me around, kissing me while I burst into tears.

"Looks like you're stuck with me for a long, long time," I joke, feeling like my future has opened up, like the clock is fixed and will keep on ticking. I think about that night under the streetlight, when Kyle assured me he was willing to be with me despite all the uncertainty cf brought to our lives. Suddenly, it didn't feel so uncertain anymore.

A few years earlier, Kyle and I had a class together at Stonehill, Introduction to Healthcare Administration, where we sat next to each other.

In order to drive home the importance of healthcare in our world, our professor talked about marriage vows during one of the first classes.

"What are the most important marriage vows?" he asked.

People raised their hands and recited different lines, until someone finally landed on it.

"In sickness and in health."

"Bingo."

Trying to nail down his point, and perhaps challenge the class in an, "I'm an adult and I know more than you," type of way, he asked: "Would you marry someone with a chronic illness? What about someone who was going to die?"

The class went quiet for a few heartbeats, and I looked around, holding my breath. Next to me, Kyle's hand shot up.

"Absolutely," he says without looking at me, staring the professor straight in the eyes.

I breathe.

Up until that point, my professor didn't know he had a student with cystic fibrosis in his class, or that her fearless boyfriend was sitting next to her. But

Kyle, still young and probably unaware of all the challenges my health would bring to our relationship, was certain from the beginning that he was ready to take them on. I sat in awe next to him, amazed that someone could be so sure, so unafraid, so committed. But that's what happens when you love someone.

One year after I took my first dose of Orkambi, what vx-770 and vx-809 came to be called, I lace up my sneakers to run the Falmouth Road Race again. This time, my lungs are clear. I can breathe, and I bound up the hills with strength and confidence. Every breath feels like a gift as I run past Nobska Light, the waves pounding the shore of the beach, the spectators with their colorful signs, and the people blasting the *Rocky* soundtrack from speakers hooked up to the bike path overhead.

I cross the finish line and look for Kyle, who has no doubt finished earlier than me thanks to his long runner's legs. I'm hoping he'll be there on bended knee, asking for my hand in marriage, but he's nowhere to be found.

"Oh well," I say. "Missed opportunity."

The next day, we pack up to go home and Kyle asks if I want to go to our favorite Italian Restaurant in Falmouth Center.

"Fine," I say. "But I have to get home and finish up my grad school paper."

I order my favorite, penne a la vodka, and Kyle gets the chicken parm.

"I can't believe how good I feel, Kyle. I'm so lucky to be able to breathe like this!"

Next, he asks if I want to go to Cupcake Charlies and grab dessert.

"Fine," I say. "But after that we actually have to go home! This paper is going to take forever."

We get inside, order a Chocolate Loves Vanilla cupcake, and sit down.

"It's cold in here," he says. "Wanna eat on the beach?"

"What?! No, Kyle. We *have* to go home. Here, we'll sit outside."

Soon, we are in the car driving home and he turns left instead of right towards the highway. He pulls up alongside the beach.

"Come on, Lau, it's beautiful outside. Let's just go toss the Frisbee around and then I promise we can go home."

I roll my eyes and get out of the car, accepting that we shouldn't waste a sunny day on Cape Cod. We walk hand in hand on the beach, watching kids splash in the waves, and families sunbathing. Finally, we get to a section where we can play Frisbee without whacking anyone in the head, since I'm such a bad catcher. Kyle hugs me from behind, his six-foot frame towering over my five, and we stand facing the water. He kisses my cheek.

"I love you so much, Lau."

"I love you, too. So, Frisbee?"

I turn around and he's on one knee, holding a box with a diamond ring.

"Lauren, will you marry me?"

I scream, and cry immediately, wailing uninterpretable words.

"Yes!"

Flash forward one more year and I'm getting off a chairlift in August. In a wedding dress, with my dad. I look at the mountains all around us and see Kyle at the end of the aisle on top of North Peak, at Sunday River. I let myself imagine this future, but never fully believed it would come. I longed for it so badly, and now here I am.

The walk down the aisle feels like an eternity. Kyle refuses to look up until I'm a few feet away from him. When he sees me, he breaks down, and I smile through tears.

When we get to our vows, I begin:

"There's a picture of us on the wall in our house with a quote that says, 'where there is great love, there are always miracles,' and this day is truly a miracle."

Just Freakin' Love Them

My story has a happy ending, but not all kids with chronic, life-threatening illnesses get to pop a pill that is going to change their life, erase their worry for the future, cause them to start contributing to their 401(k), get married, and start a future. But is anyone's story really about the ending?

Even though the hope my family and I held onto didn't prove to be a waste, my story is not about that. Though I hold a tremendous amount of thankfulness for the gift of life modern medicine has given me—whether the wishes on my candles came true or not—my story is not about the chance at a longer life.

The gift of the lessons I've learned growing up sick far outweigh the gift of a longer life. Because my family focused on showing me what a quality life meant, I have learned the ultimate lessons. I grew strong. I figured out how to gauge true crises, and I appreciate the gifts in life that everyday people take for granted. So that with each day, I can love more, give more, and relish in everyday miracles. And whether I'm granted forty more years, or two, I'll be content knowing I've lived it the best way I know how.

The love from my family is the reason I was able to learn any of these lessons. In the hard moments, it was love that got me through in the form of squeezed hands, tight hugs, and sometimes, raised voices on my behalf. And it wasn't only the love from my parents, but ultimately the love for myself that I needed in order to grow into an adult who wanted to take care of herself, who persevered, and who ultimately could be loved by my now husband,

Kyle. As a parent, all you need to do is love your child as much as you possibly can. The love that allows your child to grow isn't easy. Don't confuse love with coddling, with being too easy, or with letting them off the hook. The strong, unbreakable love is only an arm's reach away, with space in between for your sick kid to grow and learn the lessons they need to learn. And if you leave that space there, you'll grow, too.

The One Thing I Wish My Mom Did

One night, my mom and I sit sipping wine by the fireplace, chatting about how my life has turned out. It's shortly after I've started taking Orkambi, a medication already starting to clear my lungs, with the potential to change my life for the better. After we finish laughing about some dirty joke she makes, we sit in silence with the clock on the mantel ticking its familiar *tock*.

"I'm finally going to be able to sleep at night," she breathes.

She goes on to tell me about all the sleepless nights she was up worrying about me. Every cough at night, every movement, she worried. From the age of 3, to the age of 23, when I finally moved out into my own apartment. She would wonder if it was just a cough, or if something infectious was brewing in my lungs. I roll my eyes like daughters do, like I've been doing since I figured out my eyes could go that far back.

"Hey, you don't have to worry about ME!" I say, clinking my wine glass against hers.

But what I know inside, is that this mama bear loves me more than I can possible know. She took on all of my emotions, and was so strong and brave I had no idea I was supposed to be worried, or afraid, or nervous about most of what I went through. She loved me too much to allow me to be scared, so she took it on herself.

I was asked to write a guest blog post about the way my parents raised me, and was asked what they could have done differently. I thought and thought, and couldn't come up with a thing. They did all they could, and because of their support and dedication, I got through some of the toughest moments in my life.

But when my mom finally breathed a sigh of relief that night, seeing her girl healthy, I thought of one thing they could have changed: I wish they would have known that they didn't have to take on all the emotional burden. There are counselors and social workers and help out there, all they had to do was reach for it, ask for it, and take care of themselves.

I hope this book is a tiny step in that direction, to remind parents that no, it isn't easy when your kid has to grow up sick, but if you can muster up the strength to love your child, to make the tough decisions about when a good life trumps a long life, and to focus on the positive, the blessings, and the small moments—you're doing okay. It isn't a cake walk, so you have to love yourself enough to seek the resources YOU need. Just like my mom told me at the age of 11, though mine was uniquely destined to be shorter, no one life is a guarantee, we can only live it the best we can.

So give yourself permission to take care of yourself. Make a commitment to be selfish, even if it's just once a week or once a month. Pick something you have always loved to do, maybe before your child was sick, and do it. If that means you always loved to cozy up on your couch and read a book, find a quiet corner of the hospital to engross yourself in the latest romance novel while your kid takes a nap. And if you're feeling overwhelmed, like you can't do it on your own, you have *got* to ask for help. When you live in a sick kid family, the meals your friends and family dropped off when they first found out your kid was sick will slowly start to taper off. Maybe your friends stop asking how you're doing, stop coming to visit, or lose touch entirely. I guarantee, if they knew how hard you were trying to keep your head above water, they would say, "Why didn't you tell me?"

Don't be afraid to raise your hand. Don't be afraid to ask someone to throw you a life preserver. In fact, you deserve it, you need it, and you can't be expected to stay afloat without it. Whether you need your friend to take you to the spa and talk about nothing but celebrity gossip, or you need a counselor or support group to help you work through the burden on your shoulders, if you don't ask, how will they know?

Having a sick kid can wear on you, and though some days you might dig up the strength to paint a smile on your face, it isn't enough to grin and bear it every day. That isn't fair to you, when you've given up your weekly drinks with friends, your sleep, your special moments with your spouse, or time with your other children just so your sick kid will be happy. Sacrifices will be inevitable, but that doesn't mean you can't take time for self-care in between. In fact, if you find time to treat yourself every once and a while, your kid will be better off. But what will people say when you're getting a full body massage while your kid is at home with Grandma? Who the hell cares what they think. Until they've been in your shoes, they don't get to make judgements.

At the beginning of the book, I told you your child is going to grow into a tough cookie, that they'll develop a unique perspective, and most of all that they will inspire you. The same is true for you. You will inspire your child and the people around you to give love more than they take, and to be strong. You'll prove to others that they've got what it takes to face their own burdens. And at the end of the day, your bravery, your resilience, and your love will be the reason your kid is able to grow up and take on the world.

Conclusion

Although Orkambi was a life changer, it took several more years until Mom was relieved of her nursing duties to me. The drug has helped me to breathe easier and has made the day to day so much easier. I have more energy, less sinus issues, and spend less time coughing, but my lungs are still colonized with Burkholderia Cepacia, meaning I still face lung infections and require IV antibiotics. When it was time for a clean out, I moved home for two weeks at a time for Dad's home cooking and for Mom to take care of me when I needed to be hooked up to medication late at night and early in the morning, right up until I was married to Kyle.

Shortly after we got married, my lungs flared up and I needed IV antibiotics again. After talking to the doctor, I call Mom and tell her.

"And don't worry, this time Kind Kyle is taking the reins."

"Oh wow!" she says, "This will be the first time I'm not taking care of my baby! Make sure he holds your hand when you get your PICC line inserted, okay?"

"Of course, Mom. And don't worry, you're irreplaceable."

"One more thing," she adds, "Would it be okay if I call him tonight? I just want to tell him a few things.

That night, the phone rings and I hand it to Kyle. Mom gives him a breakdown of everything he needs to know for my cleanout.

"When she gets her PICC line sometimes she gets light headed. Be careful of air bubbles in the medication tubing. Take the medicine out of the fridge an hour early so it doesn't take too long to infuse. Give her the Zofran before she gets her Meropenem antibiotic because it makes her nauseous. Make sure she drinks plenty of fluids and sleeps enough. And, she'll probably ask you to hold her hand when she gets the PICC line inserted, she might break your hand off but then you're able to tell when she's in pain."

"My mama loves me alright," I say when he presses the end button.

It's 4:00AM and our alarm clock goes off, Thomas Rhett crooning from the country radio station. Kyle shoots out of bed and turns it off, carefully opening the door to go downstairs to the refrigerator. He tip-toes back into our room, puts the medicine on the bedside table, and pulls the covers up so he can sleep for another hour.

At 5:00AM, the alarm goes off again, this time it's Luke Bryan. Kyle strokes my hair and I wake up. He's standing next to the bed with a pill in his hand. I try to grab it with my index finger and thumb and he maneuvers my hand out flat, places the pill in my palm, and hands me my water bottle. After I swallow the Zofran and roll back over, he gently pulls my arm with the PICC from under the covers and hooks up the medication. I sleepily open my eyes and smile at him, and he kisses my wrist.

"Go back to sleep, you need your rest," he whispers and kisses me again, this time on the forehead.

This continues for two weeks, Kyle waking up every morning and then spending the day exhausted at work. One night before bed, as we lay staring at the ceiling, the full moon peaking in through the blinds, I say, "Kyle?"

"Mhm?"

"Thank you so much for doing this... for taking care of me."

"Lau, this is what I signed up for!"

Of course, when you love someone you are going to do everything in your power to keep them healthy and happy. When your kid grows up, you might worry about what they'll do without you, how they'll ever survive on their own. My parents worry about the same thing, but they gave me the power to be independent and to accept love. Knowing I'm able to do that allows them to sleep at night. Although the caregiver torch has been passed to my husband and me, my parents' love is still there and will always be there. That is the greatest gift they have given to me.

As a parent, it's so hard to look forward, to see that someday your kid might grow up, call you up, and tell you that they don't need you anymore. But these things remain constant: your love and your commitment to them, the lessons you've taught them, and the belief you have in them to thrive. That doesn't go away, and it will be woven into the decisions they make when it comes to their health as an adult. That is the greatest gift *you* can give.

Acknowledgments

I have been writing this book for what feels like most of my life. So I'd like to thank everyone who was there for the stories that came to life in these pages, from the time I was a little girl until the day I walked down the aisle to marry Kyle, with breath in my lungs. To my parents, Lee and John Bombardier, for always believing in me. This story is truly your story, as I wouldn't be the person I am today without you. To my brothers, Dan and Dave. I know our lives were taken up quite a bit by my issues, but you've never wavered in your support and encouragement for your little sister.

To everyone who gave me advice and encouragement along the way, especially my husband Kyle, who cooked dinner and did the dishes while I wrote many nights after work. Every single one of you who asked when my book would be done, *you* gave me the stamina to keep going.

To all my English teachers who encouraged me to write bravely and boldly, and especially to Mr. Surette, for making me fall in love with creative writing, and telling me that cystic fibrosis doesn't deserve to be capitalized.

To Professor Warren Dahlin, for showing me I had the creativity and the bravery to write my story, for encouraging me to publish it, and for reminding us not to go through the world wearing shit colored classes.

To the hardworking parents who talked to me about their experiences early on, and gave me the inspiration to write, especially Shelly Kohrmann, Amanda Leal Williams, and Adam Longwell. To every other parent who reached out to me when their child was first diagnosed, you are the reason I wrote this book, and I wish you all the best with your little ones. To my beta readers, Cindy Vinson, Rachelle Bloss, Desiree Davis, MaryAnn Waite, and Amanda Ellis, you gave me the spark I needed to accept that my story was ready for the world to read.

To my Indiegogo backers, thank you for your contributions to move this project forward. I couldn't have started without you, especially top contributors: Taryn Dickey, Mathew Edwards, Katherine, Kimberly Russell, Dave Bombardier, Sarah McNeill, Kevin Coyne, Laura Boback, John Jardin, Elizabeth (BJ) Weeks, John Martin, Annmarie Durocher, Mary Aia, Stephanie Borseti, Michael Coles, Kevin and Alli Barron, Kelly Finch, Laura Kelley Rizvi, Judy Ferbert, and my mom, Lee Bombardier.

To my formatters at Polgarus Studio, Jason and Marina Anderson, thank you for turning my words into the very thing you hold in your hands!

To my super creative cover designer Courtney Cannon at Fiction-Atlas Press, thanks for bringing Growing Up Sick to life with your gorgeous design.

And finally, to my amazing editor, Stacy Walsh. Your dedication to this story, and to making it great shines through every page.

Lauren Bombardier Weeks is *thriving* in Massachusetts with her husband, Kyle, and their Golden Retriever, Nugget. In the winter you'll find her skiing at Sunday River, Maine and in the summer you'll find her chasing the sunshine all over New England. In addition to her day job, she is a cystic fibrosis and disability advocate and shares her story and passion for life with any audience who will listen. http://thesowhatlife.com, @laurenbweeks on Instagram.

Manufactured by Amazon.ca
Bolton, ON